MAURICE

Ravel

A L I F E

MAURICE *Ravel*

A L I F E

Benjamin
Ivry

Welcome Rain Publishers

Direct any inquiries to
Welcome Rain Publishers LLC,
225 West 35th Street, Suite 1100
New York, NY 10001.

Library of Congress Cataloging-in-Publication Data
Ivry, Benjamin
    Maurice Ravel: a life / Benjamin Ivry.
        p. cm.
    Includes bibliographical references and index.
    ISBN 1-56649-152-5
        1. Ravel, Maurice, 1875-1937.   2. Composers—
    France—Biography.   I. Title.
ML410.R23 I97 2000
780'.92—dc21
[B]   00-040899

Manufactured in the United States
of America by BLAZE I.P.I.

First Edition: July 2000
1   3   5   7   9   10   8   6   4   2

To Boonkhet Hangsuwan

To the memory of Simone Boué and Emil Cioran

Contents

CONTENTS

Acknowledgments

Thanks are due to some of Ravel's younger musical contemporaries, who shared memories and thoughts about the composer: Madeleine Milhaud and Gaby Casadesus† of Paris; Hugues Cuénod of Vevey, Switzerland; David Diamond of New York; and Blanche Honegger-Moyse of Brattleboro, Vermont.

Thanks also to J. Rigbie Turner, Music Manuscripts Curator of the Pierpont Morgan Library, and Vincent Giroud, Humanities Curator of the Beinecke Library, in New Haven, Connecticut. New Yorkers who offered insights and information about Raveliana include: Catherine Anne and Jonathan Rolfe, Arbie Orenstein, Marie Ponsot, and Richard Howard. From London, Michael Rose offered astute advice.

From Alexandria, Egypt, Bernard de Zogheb was an illuminating correspondent.

At the Ravel Museum in Montfort l'Amaury, donations are accepted for much-needed restoration work, at the following address: Fondation Maurice Ravel, Le Belvédère, 5 rue Maurice Ravel, F-78490 Montfort l'Amaury, France.

Who Was Ravel?

Maurice Ravel is France's most popular composer. In August 1992, the SACEM, the French organization that calculates composers' and authors' royalties, announced that Ravel was the top French earner of royalties, more than any pop, rock, or film composer. His heirs rake in from ten to twelve million francs per year, and Ravel's work will continue to pay royalties until it falls into the public domain in the year 2012. The man who wrote *Boléro*, *Pavane pour une infante défunte*, the *Alborada del gracioso*, *Ma Mère l'Oye*, the *Rapsodie espagnole*, *L'Enfant et les sortilèges*, *L'Heure espagnole*, the piano concertos, and *Tzigane* has long been an international favorite. *Boléro* indeed merits a book in itself, for its increasingly mythical status in Hollywood and French films, such as Akira Kurosawa's *Rashomon* (1950), and Blake Edwards's 1979 comedy *10*, starring Bo Derek. In 1984 the prizewinning ice skaters Torvil and Dean danced to *Boléro* on television, and millions more became aware of the work.

Even during his lifetime, Ravel's impact was international: Earlier in the century, Arnold Bennett wrote a novel inspired by Ravel's *Miroirs,* Vaughan Williams studied with him, and Delius used his expertise as a transcriber. In the German-speaking world, Ravel had a notable encounter with Hugo von Hofmannsthal, kept up with Schoenberg and the Second Vienna school, and was written about by Theodor Adorno. In Italy he followed the experiments of the futurists in music and literature, like Ricciotto Canudo and Francesco Cangiullo, and made an impression on the composers Ildebrando Pizzetti and Gian Francesco Malipiero; in Spain, he was close to Manuel de Falla and Adolfo Salazar. America offered Ravel an interesting critical discourse from composers Virgil Thomson, Aaron Copland, and David Diamond.

One myth about Ravel is that he produced little. Other composers have produced more, and Ravel went through dry patches, but over forty years he produced some sixty works of permanent value, with virtually no weak or bad ones. It seems churlish to complain that there are "only" sixty of them. How many Vermeers are needed to make him an immortal painter? The flautist and conductor Marcel Moyse, who knew and worked with both men, thought Ravel a "genius even greater than Debussy." His range of work is extraordinary. The poet Marie Ponsot asserts that his music is admired by "an extremely wide variety of people, for many independent reasons: some who love Ravel are mainly interested in piano music, or in *mélodies,* or in orchestral works like *Boléro.* He had an intense achievement in so many different fields."

Why do we need another book about Ravel? Arbie Orenstein's two books, *A Ravel Reader* and *Ravel: Man and Musician,* present precious material, but the composer's correspondence is still little known, and the extent of Ravel's cultural influence remains to be sounded. He set up smoke screens in front of aspects of his life and work. He insisted that he was "artificial by nature," and sincere only in his insincerity. Once he told the Swiss composer Frank Martin, "An artist's greatest danger is sincerity: If we'd been sincere for even a second, we'd only have managed to have written Wagner's music."

The need for insincerity, or a lack of candor, also extends to what the composer allowed to be known about his private life. His personality and habits have retained their mystery, particularly his sexuality, a major motivation for his art. Biographers have generally avoided the subject or concluded that evidence is lacking to say whether he was heterosexual, homosexual, or asexual. In books about him, the subject of Ravel's sexuality is typically reduced to a few reluctant and unilluminating paragraphs, of no relevance to his compositions. Some friends, like the conductor Manuel Rosenthal, sincerely, if wrongly, believed that he was heterosexual, because he enjoyed talking to women prostitutes, although no one ever claimed to know of Ravel actually having sex with a woman. Yet evidence exists, in the composer's letters and in testimony from friends, for a more clearly defined portrait.

The Swiss tenor Hugues Cuénod, who knew him in the 1920s and 1930s in Paris, commented: "As for Ravel, I think that his homosexuality was sublimated, and that he was above all a 'closet queen,' of whom there are many." Yet others who knew the composer even better say Ravel was not closeted, only cagey. The American composer David Diamond, who knew Ravel from

3

1928 onward, believes that Ravel was homosexual, judging from his own impressions and from conversations with Ravel's friends, like Alexandre Tansman, who said that Ravel "very discreetly liked young men." While his parents were alive, Ravel allowed himself no public expression of his homosexual desires, and after their deaths, he stuck to his old habit of secrecy. Yet the painter Romaine Brooks, the singer Doda Conrad, and the conductor Dimitri Mitropoulos, all friends of Ravel, told Diamond that "of course" he was homosexual; other friends, like the violinist Maurice Hewitt and Emile Vuillermoz also suggested that he was gay. Basing his assessment on these reports and his own meetings with the composer, Diamond concluded that Ravel and Garbo were "the two great enigmas" who placed smoke screens around their sexuality. That Ravel was a very secretive gay man is the thesis adopted by this book.

Powerful links may be found between his hidden sexuality and his obsession with sorcery. Demonic passions forced under control were at the heart of his creative urge. His work makes repeated reference to ancient Greek sexuality, Pan, and other *fin-de-siècle* code words for homosexuality. By frankly addressing the question of his homosexuality, this book aims, more than merely to drag Ravel from his posthumous closet, to achieve a closer understanding of his motivations and works, along with a more accurate image of the man.

CHAPTER ONE

Birth to Conservatory

1875–1899

Maurice Ravel was born in 1875 in Ciboure, a small village in the Basque region of France, separated from the city of Saint-Jean-de-Luz by the Nivelle River. The first thirty-five years of the life of his mother, Marie Delouart, are a near-total blank. She was apparently born in the Basque region and spent some time in Spain, where she met Ravel's father. Biographers found that locals of Saint-Jean-de-Luz did not recall her being born there, and Manuel de Falla praised her knowledge of Spanish, which indicates that he did not take her to be a natural speaker of the language. But she would sing Spanish folk songs to Maurice, and these were a later inspiration for his work.

Basque and Spanish women usually married young, but Marie apparently did not. A romanticizing biographer, Victor Seroff, suggested that Marie might have had children before she met and married Joseph Ravel, or a secret life as a "gypsy or even a smuggler": "A woman who wanted to hurt the composer," he says, "once told him his mother's true age. Ravel was so horrified that for a long time he could not get over it." And when Seroff asked Ravel's brother, Edouard, for information about his mother's early years, Edouard said that he "saw no reason why [Seroff] should talk about their mother in a book about his brother." In any case, Ravel's mother was a violent agnostic, atypical of her time and place. As a widow, she was urged by a woman friend in Saint-Jean-de-Luz to come to church and pray; Marie said that she'd rather "be in hell with her family than in heaven all alone."

When Ravel enlisted in the army during World War I, he described his mother as a "monster" who wanted to hold onto her sons and not let them enlist to fight for their country. But, he added, she was a "monster" he loved. In spite of, or perhaps because of, her blasphemies and obscure past, Ravel was a confirmed mama's boy. The pianist Robert Casadesus recalled that his first sight of Ravel, in the early years of the century, was at a concert, tenderly holding the arm of his aged mother, helping her to her seat.

French biographers commonly assert that the fathers of great men were also great. Maurice Ravel's father, Joseph, was affectionate, with a highly developed love for music and culture, and he did not object when his son embraced an artistic career, despite the family's lack of money. Joseph Ravel was not quite the inventing genius he has been portrayed as. He tinkered with inventions in the pioneer days of automobile construction, but his most notable project was also his biggest failure. "The Whirl-wind of Death," a loop-the-loop designed for circuses and auto shows in 1906–07, was displayed at Barnum and Bailey's Circus, but it flopped either because of a fatal accident, as one story has it, or because its wooden framework was destroyed in a hurricane in Iowa in September 1907.

Joseph was born in Switzerland, and earlier branches of the family bear variants of the name on public records: But for the chance slip of a Swiss notary's pen, we might be speaking today of *Boléro* by Ravet or Ravex. A fantastic etymology of Ravel as a so-called Jewish name deriving from Rabbele [*sic*] was apparently invented by Roland-Manuel as a joke and was long afterward repeated by gullible biographers. In 1873 Joseph Ravel went to Spain as a civil engineer for a railway-construction job in the New Castille province, and there he met and married the composer's mother. After Maurice was born, another son was added to complete the family in 1879; the rather faceless Edouard was the composer's only brother. By then the family had moved to Paris, where Joseph was, as ever, seeking his fortune in industrial schemes.

The Ravel family moved frequently around Paris, trying out humble, if strenuous, business affairs. Workaholism ran in the family: After the deaths of his parents, Edouard Ravel moved into the home of his employers at a small auto-parts factory, Mr. Bonnet, and his wife. Edouard was traumatized in body and spirit by army service during World War I that turned his hair white. In later photos he looks flabby and passive, a sedentary man who adulated others, rather like Picasso's friend Jaime Sabartès. Even in adulthood, Maurice called his brother by the infantile nickname Douardouard. Ravel was known in his own circle as Rara, and the composer's friends believed that Douardouard's personality had been effaced by Rara's fame.

Regional guides claim Ravel as a Basque composer, and he would frequently return to his birthplace in later life. The seven provinces of the region are shared between France and Spain (three in France and four in Spain), and Ravel was attached to his native land, with its majestic mountain scenery and wiry, tough peasants. The Basque region is known for the sport of pelota, bullfighting, and a tradition of witchcraft and demonology. In 1608 Pierre de Lancre, a judge from Bordeaux, was named by Henri IV to investigate the troubling abundance of witches that "contaminated" the Basque country. De Lancre's report revealed that sorceries were one way of expressing forbidden sexuality: the devil, when having sex with boys or girls, "took as much pleasure in sodomy as in the most ordered and natural volup-tuousness." Male witnesses admitted performing sodomy "to please the devil," often with male relatives, one Basque man say-ing he did so "often in a passive way with [the Devil], often actively with other warlocks." Judges decided that the Basque witnesses did not really believe in the devil, but simply desired to commit adultery and sodomy, "and so they gathered, and the naughtiest one among them pretended to be Satan."

Ravel was very Basque in his use of sorcery as sexual camou-flage, returning obsessively to the theme of witchcraft as a source of inspiration. In public and even among most of his friends, Ravel suppressed his sexual desires and used witchcraft as his fore-fathers had, as an emotional safety valve and a way of expressing forbidden feelings. So long as his parents lived, according to friends who were aware of Ravel's homosexuality, he could not permit himself to express his true nature.

In Paris, the engineer Joseph Ravel enjoyed taking his sons on tours of factories, where they all admired machinery. Despite the family's money worries, Maurice had piano lessons at age seven, from Henry Ghys, a musician whose short-lived notoriety was based on the song *Air Louis XIII.* The boy also had lessons in harmony, counterpoint, and composition from Charles-René, a student of the composer Léo Delibes (who wrote the ballets *Sylvia* and *Coppélia*). Later, one of Ravel's great qualities as a composer was to produce finished works, which seem to have emerged whole from his brain. This early training in the basics of composition, at the same time as he was learning the piano, no doubt helped to develop the creative mechanism. Among his early exercises, Ravel was made to write variations on a chorale by Schumann and a theme from Edvard Grieg's *Peer Gynt.* Arbie Orenstein finds that these early efforts display "some awkward writing for the keyboard" but also have "a gentle, spontaneous lyricism."

Maurice's progress as a piano pupil must have been rapid, as he soon changed professors, moving up to the more distinguished Emile Descombes, who taught such young virtuosos as Alfred Cortot and the composer Reynaldo Hahn. When he was twelve years old, Maurice met another youngster who would be a close friend, the pianist Ricardo Viñes. Later described by Francis Poulenc as a "strange hidalgo," Viñes was a brilliant keyboard artist, much interested in romantic literature; he lent Maurice books like Aloysius Bertrand's *Gaspard de la nuit.* Viñes described the young Ravel as looking "like a Florentine page, standing straight and stiff, with bangs and flowing black hair. . . .

His delicate Basque face with its pure profile was graceful and thin atop his slender neck and narrow shoulders."

Ravel and Viñes spent hours leaning over the balcony of the Ravel family apartment on the rue Pigalle, overlooking a café where artists would gather and models would flirt with them. The boys tried to guess which model would wind up with which artist, and this early sexual sophistication belies the impression given in some biographies that Ravel was a lifelong innocent. Leaning over a balcony voyeuristically would become a typical Ravel pose, and a number of photos show the adult composer watching what is going on below, while keeping his distance from the action.

A portrait of Maurice from this time shows curly hair and large liquid eyes that might seem exaggerated if we did not know from photos that his eyes were indeed that liquidly expressive. Maurice was clearly considered the beauty of the family, taking after his mother; a portrait of Edouard, made about this time, shows a stolid, potato-faced youngster. Ravel's satisfaction in his own appearance would develop into time-consuming narcissism.

In 1889 a group of Emile Descombes's pupils, including Cortot, Hahn, and Ravel gave a public performance; Maurice played an excerpt from the Piano Concerto no. 3 by Ignaz Moscheles, a virtuoso pianist and friend of Felix Mendelssohn, who wrote eight piano concertos, of which the third, written in 1820, was the most popular for its early Romantic, pre-Chopin style. Ravel always referred to 1820 as his ideal historical period, and he would later own an Erard piano made in that year, with a dry, hard tone that doubtless influenced the works he wrote on it.

In 1889 Paris was astonished by the Eiffel Tower, built for the *Exposition Universelle,* the World's Fair that included among its attractions Rimsky-Korsakov conducting his own works, gamelan orchestras, gypsy bands, and music groups from Russia, Sudan, Serbia, and Romania. The exposition meant to show that although Europe was embroiled in an arms race, science was not only for destruction, and war "not the highest purpose of human society." The Champs de Mars below the Eiffel Tower was filled with industrial exhibits, like the *Galérie des machines,* which must have fascinated the Ravel boys. Displays offered views of distant lands and peoples, and on the Esplanade des Invalides, natives from a so-called Aissaova tribe entertained passersby by sticking their hands into flames, and piercing their tongues, eye sockets, and abdomens with spikes.

Amid such thrills, the fourteen-year-old Ravel auditioned for the Paris Conservatoire, playing the piano for faculty including the head of the institution, Ambroise Thomas, the composer of the operas *Mignon* and *Hamlet.* Although Ravel was accepted as a pupil and recognized as a gifted pianist, it was noted that he came late to class and was often distracted. He competed three times for prizes in harmony and piano but did not win. However, he enjoyed socializing with Viñes, playing four-handed piano works, and discussing favorite books. He was intrigued with Symbolist aesthetics early on, and the books he read remained important influences for the rest of his life. Ravel was secretly bookish, hiding what he read from most friends. His favorites included Villiers de l'Isle-Adam's *L'Eve future,* Barbey d'Aurevilly's *Du dandysme et de George Brummel,* and *Les Diaboliques,* J. K. Huysmans's *A rebours,* and the writings of Edgar Allan Poe as translated by Charles Baudelaire.

Villiers de l'Isle-Adam's *L'Eve future,* from 1886, is set in the laboratory of Thomas Alva Edison in Menlo Park, New Jersey, where the inventor laments that his phonograph arrived too late to capture history's key moments. Edison builds a female robot, Hadaly, from wires with "two phonographs of gold" for lungs, and a cylinder on which her gestures are recorded. Ever fascinated with machines, Ravel later toyed with setting E.T.A. Hoffmann's story of the mechanical doll Olympia.

Barbey d'Aurevilly, another of Ravel's favorite authors, lived with the writer Jean Lorrain, who was called "Jehanne la bonne Lorraine," a jokingly camp reference to Joan of Arc. Both liked to wear makeup and elaborate costumes, with Lorrain piling on the jewelry, tinting his moustache with henna and gold powder, and signing newspaper articles "Mimosa" and "Stendhaletta." In *A un diner d'athées,* a novella from Barbey's collection *Les Diaboliques,* a sadist named Major Ydow, who looks like an emerald-eyed bust of Antinous, the Emperor Hadrian's companion, seals up his lover Rosalba's sexual organs with boiling wax. In another, "La Vengeance d'une femme," a duchess-turned-prostitute plies her trade in Ravel's home area of Saint-Jean-de-Luz, which must have given the boy a thrill. *Du Dandysme et de George Brummel* made an even greater impression on the young Maurice, who began to look and act like a dandy, as that breed was defined by Baudelaire, Huysmans, and Barbey d'Aurevilly himself. Since almost every reminiscence of Ravel would cite his dandylike appearance, it is important to explore the sources for this consciously fabricated personality which lasted his whole life.

In Barbey's essay on Brummel, the dandy's features are described: glacial wit; the appearance of total self-control; sober and rigid elegance; an ability to wound others with words and ignore his victims' discomfort. Ravel would later conform to this behavior in social situations, inspired by eighteenth-century British dandies like Brummel or Horace Walpole.

Ravel drew some elements of his persona as dandy from the works of Edgar Allan Poe, as translated by Baudelaire. Jean-Paul Sartre suggested that Baudelaire's myth of the dandy conceals not homosexuality, but exhibitionism. Yet Oscar Wilde and other gay writers advanced a tradition of the androgynous dandy. The essayist Jules Lemaître noted, "The dandy has something against nature, something androgynous with which he can endlessly seduce."

Huysmans called another of Ravel's favorite books, the novel *A rebours*, "vaguely clerical, a bit pederastic," and its chief character, des Esseintes, a "Christian and pederast, impotent man and unbeliever." The effeminate des Esseintes provided a role model to a generation of aesthetes and dandies who, like him, retired to their neurotic collections of books and artworks. Viñes once referred to Ravel's "mixture of medieval Catholicism and satanic impiety," which is closer to a description of des Esseintes than to the agnostic Ravel.

To young Maurice, Poe was a double influence, not just as a dandy but also as a creative theorist. He cited Poe's essay, "The Philosophy of Composition," as the most important lesson he ever received about composing. In it, Poe stated, "Every plot, worth the name, must be elaborated to its *dénouement* before anything be attempted with the pen." This became Ravel's approach to composition, thinking everything out in his head before setting pen to paper. It presumed an intense mental effort and constant pressure, conscious and unconscious, during the creative act. Poe described his writing of "The Raven" step by step "with the precision and rigid consequences of a mathematical problem." Ravel liked to tell students, "I do logarithms," to arrive at compositional solutions. Both Poe and Ravel assumed this pseudoscientific posture as a way of disciplining creative frenzy that they feared otherwise might go uncontrolled; the need for discipline in creativity obsessed both men.

They also agreed about the ideal length of creative works. In an essay Ravel treasured, "The Poetic Principle," Poe maintained that a poem can only sustain its excitement for a half-hour, "at the very utmost." With few exceptions, this was also the time-limit of Ravel's compositions, if only to make it possible for him to hold an entire work in his head before setting it down on paper. Poe stressed that beauty was more important in poetry than truth, which was better suited to prose. Ravel would often insist that in any artwork, beauty was paramount.

While mulling over such artistic questions, he continued his studies. In February 1893, while he was still at the Conservatoire, Ravel went with Viñes to pay homage to a musical hero, Emmanuel Chabrier. The two teenagers were cordially received, and Chabrier listened carefully to their playing of his *Trois valses romantiques,* but interrupted them so often with conflicting and varied criticisms that they left his home "completely bewildered." Chabrier noted in his address book: "Ravel (M. Maurice) pianist, 73 rue Pigalle," but a week later he had an attack of paralysis that prevented further contacts. Later, Ravel would also perplex students who came to play his works with unexpected opinions and advice. At about the same time, Maurice met Erik Satie through his father, who knew the Montmartre composer, then eking out a living as pianist at the Café de la Nouvelle Athènes. Satie gravely consulted with Ravel and Viñes about his plan to set newspaper advertisements to music, writing miniscule orchestrations to texts from the want ads.

In 1893 Ravel wrote the piano piece *Sérénade grotesque,* much influenced by Chabrier, and the song *Ballade de la Reine morte d'aimer* in the Satie vein. *Sérénade grotesque,* marked "very pizzicato," was the first of Ravel's portraits of a grotesque, tragicomic persona fitting awkwardly into the role of lover. The *Ballade de la Reine morte d'aimer,* set to a poem by the Belgian writer Roland de Marès (1874–1955), was a mournful ditty, with its "little bells of Thulé" that play a "supreme Hosanna" for a Bohemian queen.

The following spring, Ravel met the composer Edvard Grieg at the Montparnasse apartment of friends, where Ravel played Grieg's *Norwegian Dances* on the piano. Grieg stopped him, saying, "No, young man, not like that at all. . . . It's a peasant dance." Ravel started to play again and Grieg leaped around the room in an authentic peasant dance, creating a memorable scene of an elfin pianist and a tiny troll dancer.

In August 1895, Ravel returned to composition with a setting of "Un grand sommeil noir," a poem by Paul Verlaine, which remained unpublished during the composer's lifetime. He set only two poems by Verlaine, who was much more the poet of Debussy and Fauré, and *Un grand sommeil noir* starts off in a sunless Mussorgsky mood, describing in bass notes how a "vast dark sleep falls on my life." Ravel's first significant piano work, the

Habanera for two pianos, was finished in November 1895 and later given orchestral form as the third movement of *Rapsodie espagnole*. In the same month, Ravel wrote his first published work, *Menuet antique*. The title is a paradox, uniting an eighteenth-century dance to an ancient Greek sensibility. The *Menuet antique* is saucy, like a naughty Fragonard painting, rococo yet with earthy passion. A pounding, pulsing rhythm of Pan's dance is given to harmonies that sound tantalizingly like those of Bach's *Chaconne*.

The lore of Pan permeated Ravel's work from this early *Menuet antique* through *Daphnis et Chloé* and beyond. The published musical score of *Menuet antique* showed an image of a bare-chested Pan playing his pipes. Ancient Greek imagery in art represented for the generation of Decadents a revival of the Arcadian tradition, including sexual freedom. In Arcadia, Pan expressed violent sexuality through music. The ancient Greeks used the expression "to honor Pan" to mean male homosexual activity, and Panic love, like Panic fear, was violent, sudden, and unforeseen. Dance and music were essential occupations of this animalistic leaper, deformed and unhappy in love, whose music could be irresistibly charming. Panic fear was often present in armies during wartime, and all-night initiatory festivals of Pan were marked by special cries and music to exorcise fears and phantoms. Deeply imbued with this mythological lore, Ravel's works often embody the Panic ideal.

Ravel finished two more songs in December 1896: *"Sainte,"* set to a poem by Stéphane Mallarmé, and *D'Anne jouant de l'espinette,* to words by Clément Marot. *Sainte,* which was published only in 1907, is like a soft-toned Puvis de Chavannes portrait of a woman saint. The writer Vladimir Jankélévitch saw *Sainte* as evidence of Ravel's "esoteric" period, influenced by Satie's Rosicrucian music. *Sainte* is atypically simple and direct and may have been intended as an homage to his mother as domestic saint, a "female musician of silence" as he called her. Ravel often stated how vital was his mother's quietly loving presence, calling her his "only reason for living." The song sounds unusually sincere, given that Ravel was already formulating his self-image as insincere dandy.

The two works written in 1897, *Sonate pour Violon et Piano* in one movement, and *Entre cloches,* for two pianos, show the influence of Gabriel Fauré and César Franck. *Entre Cloches* was joined to *Habanera* to make up the two-movement *Sites auriculaires.* Meaning literally "places which can be sensed by the ear," the title sounds medical, echoing Satie's parodic titles. Ravel enjoyed surgical-sounding expressions, especially if they also had a potentially erotic ring; eating cherries one day, he told the pianist Gaby Casadesus they were a "buccal pleasure." The *Habanera* begins tentatively, as if timidly knocking on the door. There is a comic disjunction between the proud Spanish themes and the mock-shy way they are treated, rhythmic passages presented with hesitation, as if they needed to be obstinately learned. This approach, akin to the humor of Chabrier and Satie, is at several ironic removes from Spain.

The *Sonate pour Violin et Piano* in one movement is about fourteen minutes long, written in the style of the Franck. Ravel had not yet developed the theory that the piano and violin were "essentially incompatible," and the early sonata is full-hearted, lush music on exalted heights of emotion.

In autumn 1897, Ravel was offered a job teaching music in Tunisia, which he turned down in order to stay close to his family and friends. Not going to North Africa meant opportunities missed for personal development and for a full investigation of Arab themes. Ravel's fascination with such subjects was always at a remove. Undiluted experience with the Arab world might not have offered him the artificiality he craved.

One danger of real contacts with North Africa was illustrated by Camille Saint-Saëns, Fauré's teacher, who was plagued by blackmailing letters from North African men he paid, apparently too little, for sex. Saint-Saëns received a series of such letters, like one in 1893 from a young Algierian named Victor Dumesnil: "Maybe there are pederasts of your kind in Paris whom you support with bits of bread, but it won't be the same with me. . . . You're a liar, a thief, and a pederast." Ravel would avoid this kind of experience, common at the time.

Meanwhile, a faculty shake-up at the Conservatoire had resulted in the resignation of Jules Massenet as professor of composition, and the hiring of Gabriel Fauré to fill his place. At the time, Fauré was still considered a radical, whose works were of spiky difficulty to traditionalists. Still tinkering at his *Requiem,* which he wrote "for pleasure," Fauré was an open-minded and warm teacher. Very much of his time, Fauré still managed to keep a certain independence that would prove a good model for his most famous pupil. Although he admired Wagner and made a pilgrimage to Bayreuth, Fauré allowed no audible influences from the German composer to enter his music. At the turn of the century, Fauré remained stubbornly devoted to writing intimate chamber works, even when most of his contemporaries sought larger-scale canvases for self-expression. Never abandoning the quality of tender intimacy, Fauré's works remain among the most endearing of modern French music, and Ravel would certainly learn from this example. Yet some of Fauré's later works, particularly the ones for piano solo, retain a mystical quality that transcends mere Gallic charm. Ravel was happy to join Fauré's class in 1898, and in a typical anecdote that he enjoyed repeating, Fauré at first rejected one of his works, then asked Ravel to bring the work to class again. When he asked why, the teacher's answer came: "I might have been wrong." Fauré's pupils included Georges Enesco, Charles Koechlin, and Raoul Laparra, and Ravel would dedicate to Fauré such later works as *Jeux d'eau* and his string quartet. Even after Ravel was definitively excluded from the list of students at the Conservatoire in 1900, he continued to audit Fauré's class until 1903. He also carried on his private lessons in counterpoint and orchestration with André Gédalge, who taught fugue as well, counting among his students Arthur Honegger, Darius Milhaud, and Florent Schmitt. Ravel later wrote that Gédalge was the first to make him realize the importance of structure in composition, and of technique, not just as a "scholastic abstraction." With an unusually clear teaching method, Gédalge focused mainly on the works of Bach and Mozart, at a time when this was uncommon.

In his first year under the new regime at the Conservatoire, Ravel wrote two songs, *Chanson du rouet,* to a poem by Leconte de Lisle, and *Si morne,* after Emile Verhaeren. *Chanson du rouet* [Spinning song] is in the tradition of Saint-Saëns's *Rouet d'Omphale* and Schubert's *Gretchen at the Spinning Wheel,* but it is hampered by a weak text. *Si Morne* is heavy with Symbolist depression, describing a "mouth acrid with molds . . . Rotting, hugely swaddled in ennui." Ravel set this text with urgency, perhaps as an expression of his stiflingly overprotected home life.

The same year, 1898, saw his first work written for full orchestra, the overture, *Shéhérazade*. The *1001 Nights* provided for the composer an atmosphere of Eastern sexual liberation, among other things. A number of stories in the collection joke about homosexuality, particularly the comic pederast Abu Nuwas, also one of the great Arab poets, while other characters like to "eat both figs and pomegranates," a metaphor for bisexuality. Gérard Pirlot has written about Sheherazade's essential "perversity," using words to achieve unconscious occult powers at night. Talking all night, Sheherezade saved herself and a king who was wounded by a wife's infidelity with a "well-hung black slave more viril than he," Pirlot explains, "on whom he projects fantasies of passive homosexuality." As for Ravel, he would tell friends, "I only begin to live at night," and as a nocturnal creature, he used music for some of the magical purposes Sheherezade aimed at with words.

Whatever his desires for liberation, at the Conservatoire Ravel was an exuberant joker. He would breeze into the classroom in the teacher's absence and strike up a parody on the piano, setting the words from the aria "Pourquoi me reveiller?" from Massenet's *Werther* to the tune of "Tarara boom-de-ay!," a turn-of-the-century hit. "Tarara boom-de-ay!" had a naughty reputation, sung at cabarets where girls tossed up their skirts, and Rara was a fan of this song, which contained his nickname in its title.

On March 5, 1898, Ravel had his public début as a composer with a performance of *Sites Auriculaires* at a concert sponsored by the Société Nationale de Musique. Reading from the score, the performers Viñes and Marthe Dron came to grief during the technically challenging *Entre cloches* section. Another significant premiere followed in April, when Viñes played the *Menuet antique* in a recital of new music. Fauré occasionally took his students along to posh salons, like that of Madame René de Saint-Marceaux, where Debussy, André Messager, and Vincent d'Indy were also present. Madame de Saint-Marceaux mused over the impassive Ravel in her diary: "Is he pleased to hear his music? You cannot tell. What an odd fellow." Ravel was once obliged to improvise at the piano when the American dancer Isadora Duncan performed, an experience he did not enjoy. In August 1898, Ravel wrote to Madame de Saint-Marceaux, referring to himself as a "musical Alcibiades." The French historian Henry Houssaye described Alcibiades as a lovely young man surrounded by perverse male friends who wanted to have sex with him, but he only accepted love from one man, Socrates. Ravel, in referring to himself as Alcibiades, or "Alkibiade," as he spelled it, did not specify who his Socrates was. But his favorite *Du Dandysme et de George Brummel* stated that dandies were "Androgynes of history, no longer of Fable, among whom Alcibiades was the most beautiful."

Another salon Ravel attended was hosted by Winnaretta Singer, an American sewing-machine heiress and lesbian who had married the gay Prince Edmond de Polignac. The Princesse de Polignac later commissioned many fine composers, including Stravinsky, Falla, and Milhaud. Ravel was to come early on the list with the *Pavane pour une infante défunte* in 1899.

In 1898 Ravel and Ricardo Viñes met the Symbolist painter Odilon Redon at the home of a mutual friend, and a friendship was born. As an adult, Viñes became a student of the mystic arts,

21

graphology, palmistry, and number symbolism, in which he may have involved Ravel. He wrote a poem about number symbolism, inspired by Rimbaud's "Voyelles," assigning colors to letters; he also liked to quote Saint Augustine: "In the world, everything is merely numbers, weight, and measure." As a royalist, Viñes cast the horoscope of King Louis XVII, the unacknowledged heir to the French throne, and belonged to a sect called The Saviors of Louis XVII, which believed that the Orléans family, who declared themselves heirs to the throne, were "evil incarnate." Viñes was an avid reader of mystics like Blanc de Saint-Bonnet who were obsessed by the myth of the Divine Androgyne, uniting male and female elements.

Ravel's friends Déodat de Sévérac and Michel Calvocoressi were also devotees of palmistry and had their fortunes told by Paris mediums like Madame Fraya and Madame de Thèbes, later credited with predicting World War I. Ravel, with his Basque background of witchcraft and its repercussions, fit easily into the Symbolist quest for magic and the ideal androgyne, as depicted in the art works of Odilon Redon. Viñes noted in his journal on May 21, 1898: "I went to Ravel's home and proposed to take him to Fabre's to see Redon's pastels, and surprise! . . . Redon showed up in person! Fabre introduced us. Redon told me to come see him! Ravel was dead with admiration in front of the pastels, which are marvellous."

Redon's painting *The Red Tree* (ca. 1905, in a Paris private collection) shows a clean-shaven man resembling Ravel; he wears "an initiate's cap" and stares with infantile concentration at a tree. The tree's mostly bare branches have white cottony blossoms on them; although there is no proof that Redon had Ravel's face in mind when painting his initiate, the fascination with trees and flowers coincides with the composer's own nature obsessions. From the time of their meeting, Redon was a frequent guest, along with Ravel and Viñes, at the home of the art collector Cyprien Godebski. Known as Cipa, Godebski was later remembered as the brother of Misia Godebska, the flamboyant muse of painters like Bonnard and Vuillard, and a friend of Diaghilev's. Misia would later marry Alfred Edwards, a newspaper tycoon, and then the mural painter J. M. Sert, whence the name she has become best known by to posterity, Misia Sert.

In 1899 Ravel wrote a second song after a poem by Clément Marot, *D'Anne qui me jecta de la neige*. The two Marot settings were joined as *Epigrammes de Clément Marot*. The first, about Anne throwing snow at her lover, communicates piano harmonies with concentrated heat, like burning coals. The other song, *D'Anne jouant de l'espinette*, begins with a dainty dance to evoke the eighteenth century. The composer Charles Koechlin recalled that Ravel played this piano part with special charm. Its liquid grace is matched by a seductive vocal line. He also completed *Pavane pour une infante défunte*, for piano, which was later orchestrated; the composer intended its graceful melody to be played extremely slowly, more slowly than almost any modern interpretation. The title, Pavane for a Dead Infanta, was chosen for its euphony rather than any specific meaning; this allowed Ravel to quip when he heard one dispirited, lifeless rendition that it was the princess who was supposed to be defunct, not the pavane. One infanta was still remembered in Saint-Jean-de-Luz during Ravel's childhood. King Louis XIV married the Spanish Infanta Marie-Thérèse d'Autriche there in 1660, and the Maison de l'Infante, the house where the Infanta stayed before the ceremony, was still extant in Ravel's day.

Another Infanta appears in Ravel's beloved *Les Diaboliques:* In the novella *Le Rideau cramoisi,* an enigmatic, disdainful mistress is likened to Velázquez's *Infanta with Spaniel.* Whatever the source of Ravel's pavane, its charm is timeless, like that of the so-called Bach Air on the G String or Pachelbel's *Kanon.* Like these other tops of the classical pops, it has sustained criticism, not least from the composer himself who was suspicious of its popularity, yet it is uncorrupted by its fame.

That winter, at a dress rehearsal for the Concerts du Conservatoire, Ravel was introduced to the soprano Jane Bathori, an important interpreter of modern song and a fine pianist who accompanied herself in recitals. Bathori was to premiere a number of Ravel songs, including the *Histoires naturelles, Trois poèmes de Stéphane Mallarmé, Chansons madécasses,* and *Rêves.*

Meanwhile, in May 1899, a concert at the Société Nationale de Musique had included Ravel's overture *Shéhérazade,* which the composer conducted in his first appearance at the podium. The work is essentially eastern dance music, with an Asian-Russian lilt in the Borodin style—ardently romantic music with full use of the orchestral palette. Although it had a mixed reception, approvers outweighed dissenters. The critic Henri Gauthier-Villars, known as "Willy," was one of the naysayers. As the husband of Colette, Willy was known for locking his wife in her room until she produced essays and books which he would sign with his own name. Willy, or one of his amanuenses, called Ravel's overture "a jarring début, an inept plagiarism of the Russian school (Rimsky faked by a Debussy-ite who is straining to reach the level of

Satie)." Willy trotted out his cutting wit again at a January 1900 concert in which Ravel's *Epigrammes de Clément Marot* were sung; he declared them "pleasant, but no more than that, not revealing [in French, 'ne ravélant pas' made for an excruciating pun] a very individual personality. Let's wait."

Ravel would not have long to wait before recognition of his mastery came.

CHAPTER TWO

Les Apaches

1900–1907

By the turn of the century, Ravel had acquired skill as a composer but had still not broken free from the Conservatoire. In 1900 he began a six-year struggle with the academic authorities in his attempt to win the prestigious Prix de Rome, awarded annually by the Académie des Beaux Arts to a promising composition student who then spent four years at the Villa Medicis in Rome. Past winners included Hector Berlioz in 1830, Charles Gounod in 1839, Georges Bizet in 1857, Jules Massenet in 1863, and Claude Debussy in 1884. Although writing fugues and a cantata to a required text of little poetic value didn't attract Ravel, winning the Prix de Rome meant career advancement, and the young composer did not have the money to ignore such an imperative. He dutifully entered the competition five times and failed on each occasion. The first time, in May 1900, he was eliminated right away, and when he entered the fugue contest again in July, he received a zero from the Conservatoire director,

Théodore Dubois, who found the entry "impossible, due to terrible errors in writing." Orenstein confirms that Ravel's entries contained "several academic infractions." After losing two fugue competitions, he was expelled from Fauré's composition class but nevertheless was permitted to audit the class until 1903.

As a consolation for these failures, in 1900 Ravel began to spend time in an informal all-male social group known as the *Apaches*. This name was ironic, as real Parisian *Apaches* were lowlife hoodlums who beat their girlfriends and stole for a living. Ravel's group was a bunch of young male aesthetes, some of them exquisite indeed. According to one story, the name *Apaches* was found when they were hurrying down a street and brushed by a news-vendor, who exclaimed, "Hey, watch out, you *Apaches!*" Out of sheer inappositeness, the name stuck. One of the group, Maurice Delage, stated that their "cardinal rule" was to "keep women out of the place as much as possible." Women were generally rejected not just as romantic objects, but also as musicians. Ravel wrote in April, 1901 to Florent Schmitt, "I have always considered a woman who writes fugues to be something of a hermaphrodite."

The *Apaches* included the poets Léon-Paul Fargue and Tristan Klingsor, the long-haired young *abbé* Léonce Petit, known as "The Curly-locks of Loyola," the conductor Désiré-Emile Inghelbrecht, Ricardo Viñes, and the composers André Caplet, Manuel de Falla, Florent Schmitt, and Déodat de Sévérac. Ravel would sometimes entertain the group by dressing up as a ballerina, complete with tutu and falsies, and dancing on pointe, his beard contrasting with his tiny, wiry form, much like the body of a real ballerina. Viñes recalled that Ravel's friends were "convulsed" by these shows.

Among the only woman to socialize with them occasionally was Jane Mortier, the pianist wife of Ravel's friend Robert Mortier. Group photos from the early *Apache* days show the obese Jane Mortier seated at the piano. Even in days when rounded figures were appreciated in Paris, Jane was not an erotic threat to the bachelors' group. Tristan Klingsor recalled that Ravel, usually so courteous, was extremely rigid about the no-women-allowed policy because he "insisted on eluding the hook." When a woman singer "of great talent and a sharp customer" set her heart on Ravel, he soon sent her packing. Klingsor made a reference to this woman as being Jewish (*"elle en fut pour son hebreu"*), and it is possible the lady in question was Emma Bardac, a French Jewish singer who used to be the lover of Fauré and went on to become the second Mrs. Claude Debussy. In any case, Klingsor remembered that she "didn't lack wit and told the story on herself, laughing about it." Ravel later dedicated his song *"l'Indifférent"* to Emma Bardac, perhaps as an explanation of his indifference to her sexual advances.

Like other secret societies, the *Apaches* had their codes and passwords. To escape unpleasant encounters, Ravel invented a fictional friend, Gomez de Riquet, with whom an appointment was a pretext for escape. Roger Nichols has plausibly suggested that this may have been in imitation of Oscar Wilde's Bunbury in *The Importance of Being Earnest*. A whistled melody from Borodin's Second Symphony also served as a code rallying cry for the group. It was to this assembly of friends that Rara would give the first performances of piano works like *Jeux d'eau, Oiseaux tristes,* and the Sonatine.

At this time Ravel's appearance was exotic, as the pianist Maurice Dumesnil recalled: "I can still visualize his high stiff collar and Lamartine tie, and the side whiskers which gave him the aspect of an Austrian diplomat." In society he met writers like Henri de Régnier, Paul Valéry, Léon Blum, and Franc-Nohain. Blum was described by Jules Renard as "a beardless young man with the voice of a girl, who can recite for two hours by the clock from Pascal, La Bruyère, Saint-Evremond, etc." Decades later, he would become the Socialist President of France and would continue to enjoy Ravel's music.

The closest of these friends, the poet Léon-Paul Fargue, met Ravel in 1902 at the home of a Decadent aesthete, Paul Sordès, a painter who admired Whistler and Aubrey Beardsley. Fargue was still smarting from a much-publicized sexual affair with the tiny, muscle-bound Alfred Jarry, the author of *Ubu Roi* and *Supermâle*. Fargue met Jarry around 1892, when they were both in school, and a class photo shows the two together. The teenaged Fargue has a pompadour haircut and a wide, feminine, tabby-cat face, looking rather like Colette. Jarry would concoct bizarre compliments for Fargue, comparing his lover's eyes to "niggers' penises." They broke up in 1895, but the Jarry-Fargue affair made such an impression in literary circles that two years later, Louis Lormel published a satirical short story, "Entre soi," in the literary review *La Plume:* Jarry and Fargue appear under the names Death's Head and Androgyne, respectively. In retaliation, Jarry wrote a story in which Lormel, called Lermoul (or "their idiot") is depicted as "a hideous, half-dead, and putrified creature feeding on its own excrements." Fargue never mentioned his gay experiences in writing, although he scarcely needed to, given Jarry's vocal posturing as a nightmare ex-lover. Whether or not Fargue's friendship with Ravel included sex, he must have been relieved at Ravel's tightlipped manner about eros, compared to Jarry's exhibitionistic hysteria. Ravel's wiry smallness may have physically recalled Jarry but was certainly less threatening than the *Supermâle*.

Some friends, like Vuillermoz, would later cast Léon-Paul Fargue in the Socratic role of loving counseler to Ravel. For Vuillermoz, it was Fargue's advice that kept Ravel from becoming too precious in his artistic taste. Without it, the composer was prone to go overboard with eccentric judgments, like declaring the overrefined Honoré d'Urfé the greatest French poet. As for Fargue, he compared Ravel to Leonardo da Vinci; the turn-of-the-century French view of Leonardo was epitomized in an 1865 essay by Hippolyte Taine that described him as a "spritual androgyne" who had "something quite delicate, quite soft, almost feminine." Taine also remarked on Leonardo's "nearly maternal love" for his male students and the androgyny of a painting like *St. John the Baptist.*

In 1901 Ravel continued to audit Fauré's class at the Conservatoire, entered a composition contest which he did not win, and failed in another try at the Prix de Rome. He wrote a cantata to an assigned text and only placed third; as he informed Lucien Garban in a July 1901 letter, he was told by a professor that he had "a melodic faucet in a place you will permit me not to specify, from which music flows effortlessly." From the same source, however, and in the same year, flowed *Jeux d'eau,* the most important of his early piano works. Usually seen as a statement of musical impressionism, *Jeux d'eau* has clear antecedents in works by Franz Liszt, such as *Les jeux d'eau à la Villa d'Este,* but also foreshadows works to come, like Debussy's *Jardins sous la pluie.* The piece uses piano techniques like trills and a glissando that slides along the black keys down to the very bottom of the keyboard. The composer's message was about the total freedom and joy that comes from mastering artistic discipline. Unusually impressionistic in Ravel's *oeuvre,* the original score quoted a line by the poet Henri de Régnier (1864–1936): "A river god laughing at the water that tickles him." In photos the bearded and jovial Joseph Ravel resembled Neptune, and Ravel may have written this work with his father in mind.

When *Jeux d'eau* was premiered by Viñes at the same concert as the original piano version of the *Pavane pour une infante défunte,* some critics, like Saint-Saëns, found it "cacophony," and it pleased the audience less than the *Pavane.* Today, however, it is generally seen today as more musically significant. Ravel tended to dismiss the *Pavane* for its relative lack of development, although he did orchestrate it in 1910.

In 1902, Debussy's *Pelléas et Mélisande* premiered. Ravel attended repeatedly with fascination, although Fargue's claim that the *Apaches* were present at each of the first forty performances probably should not be taken literally. Ravel's first personal contacts with Claude Debussy likely occurred in 1898. No letters between the two men have come to light, but the mentions of Ravel in Debussy's letters to others are always a bit irritated. Ravel, for his part, admired Debussy enormously as a composer, later saying that he would like to hear *L'Après-midi d'un faune* if he were dying. But he admitted that it was perhaps fated that he and Debussy should be on "cold" terms, since the older musician was always quick to take offense about career matters. It is natural that posterity has linked Debussy and Ravel together closely,

31

as two French composers, among their country's greatest, who were contemporaries. Yet their music sounds distinctly unalike. Debussy was often impressionistic, and Ravel rarely so, preferring a hard-edged and smart, rhythmic pulse. One cannot imagine Debussy writing a comic opera like *L'Heure espagnole,* and when Ravel did create dreamy moments, in his touchingly poetic *L'Enfant et les sortilèges,* they were unlike the dream world of *Pelléas et Mélisande.* Academia has produced far more books about Debussy than Ravel; the elder composer is honored each year with a massive yearbook of studies, while the equivalent publication for Ravel is a relatively wispy and occasional affair. It is best for today's listeners to follow the example of the two composers during their own lifetimes and keep them separate, even if record companies pair up their works on CDs as a marketing ploy.

In 1902 Ravel had a third shot at the Prix de Rome with the cantata *Alcyone,* but the top prize went to another composer, Aymé Kunc, who left no memorable compositions, though he went on to a respectable career as director of the Toulouse conservatory. The same year, Frederick Delius, who had recently settled in France, hired Ravel to arrange a piano-vocal score of his opera *Margot la Rouge.* Ravel was not influenced by this brush with Delius, who later wrote some scathing letters about the younger man's music, but instead pursued his own course with the first movement of a string quartet which he entered for a composition prize in January 1903. The competition's judge, Théodore Dubois, thought it "lacked simplicity," but Ravel finished the quartet anyway, and followed it with his song cycle *Shéhérazade.* He also made another try at the Prix de Rome with the cantata *Alyssa.* The award went to Raoul Laparra, a Basque composer of some talent, later displayed in his opera *L'Illustre Fregona.*

Ravel's continued lack of success with the Prix de Rome, and with practically all competitions he entered, was to some degree his own fault. Like Berlioz before him, he found the assigned texts uninspiring and not worth the effort required. In 1903 he entered again, although he was busy with his own works, a *Sonatine* for piano, and a song, *Manteau de fleurs,* to a poem by Paul Gravollet. Once again he failed to win a prize. *Manteau de Fleurs* is an obsessive listing of flowers that are pink, with something of the repetition given to the color green in Schubert's *Die Schöne Müllerin.* Amid the brilliant pink bouquet, "lilies have the right to be white," and a mournful chord brings death into nature, as the snake enters the Garden of Eden, a frequent theme in Ravel's work.

Sonatine, dedicated to Cipa Godebski and his wife, Ida, is in three movements, marked "Modéré," "Mouvement de Menuet," and "Animé," lasting a total of about twelve minutes. It represents an advance on *Jeux d'eau* because although water still flows, emotion appears amid the jets, not miniaturist in effect. After the deliberate first movement, the minuet is decisive and forward-moving, a brainy dance with French eighteenth-century wit. (Some of Ravel's friends asserted that he "looked like Voltaire," thinking of the affectionately comic portraits by the Swiss painter Jean Huber of the spry, rail-thin philosopher stepping into his pants or kicking a horse.)

Another side of Ravel's appearance in his *Apache* days is powerfully evoked in a 1902 oil portrait by Henri Manguin, a painter mostly known for his nudes and his relationship with the Fauves. The portrait has a startlingly Luciferian aspect, with swarthy skin, thick sensual features, and a devilish eye. The "stinger" beard and brooding, sardonic smirk suggest an ancestor of Frank Zappa. While painting, Manguin often whistled themes from Beethoven's 5th and 9th symphonies, which would have raised a grimace from Ravel, who loathed the composer he called "the Big Deaf One." This is a dark, sensual Ravel, resembling Viñes's description of "satanic impiety," but rarely seen in photos or other portraits, where he usually looks self-contained. The only other image of Ravel with this force is an impromptu photo taken years later, in which he grimaces and twists his body like a goblin shaking hands with the violinist Jacques Thibaud.

In 1904 Ravel's string quartet had its first performance in Paris to mixed reviews, although it later became an international calling card. When the Kneisel Quartet played it in Boston on December 6, 1906, the *Boston Evening Transcript* called the work the best in its form since Debussy: "Rarely does a string quartet by an almost unknown composer leave behind such pursuing memories as did Maurice Ravel's after the Kneisels had played it on Tuesday. . . . The harmonic distinction of the music made it sound as no music of its kind has sounded since Debussy's quartet." In one of those anecdotes biographers find irresistible, Debussy supposedly told the younger man, "In the name of the gods of music, and in my name, don't change anything in your quartet." No source actually verifies this praise, however.

Whatever Debussy may have said, the quartet is supple, light, and delicately tender. This modest, intimate art is like an interior by Edouard Vuillard, yet Mendelssohnian in its flighty little figures ready to take off at a moment's notice. Its melodies are quintessentially French, like the songs of his master, Fauré, and the quartet was a statement of calm, harmonious affection for his teacher's idiom after he left the class, a prodigal son extending his arms to be embraced by the forgiving parent.

Also in 1904 came a much-discussed scandal in the private life of Claude Debussy, when he left his wife, Lilly, who had stuck by him in tough times, to live with his mistress, Emma Bardac. Distraught, Lilly shot herself in the chest, which did not change Debussy's decision to leave her. All Debussy's friends were shocked by his "inhuman" behavior, his only defenders being Satie, the critic Louis Laloy, and a Swiss linguist friend, Robert Godet. A collection was organized to help the destitute Lilly, and everyone who knew the couple participated, including Debussy's future biographer René Peter, the conductor André Messager, the soprano Mary Garden, and the poet Pierre Loüys. In her memoirs, Misia Sert misleadingly said that she, the soprano Lucienne Bréval, and Ravel "settled a pension" on Lilly and that Debussy "never forgave her" for this action. Ravel had no money to pay alimony to other men's wives, although he may have participated once in the general collection. Musicologist François Lesure explained that Debussy was angry with Ravel for a joking remark the younger man made on the occasion of his marriage to Emma Bardac; this story seems more typical of both men.

A graver subject of general discussion was the Dreyfus Affair, which caused a violent international polemic for over a decade. In 1894 Captain Alfred Dreyfus, a Jewish officer in the French army, was arrested for treason and accused of having sold military secrets. Despite public outcry that the real guilt was elsewhere, Dreyfus was sent to Devil's Island. In 1899 he was retried and again found guilty, though this time with "extenuating circumstances." Intellectuals and artists were outraged, and Edvard Grieg refused to visit France on a concert tour because of his horror "at the contempt with which justice is treated" in France. Yet some artists and intellectuals were against Dreyfus, out of patriotism, love of the army, and anti-Semitism: the royalist Ricardo Viñes was a rabid anti-Dreyfusard, as was the anti-semitic Vincent d'Indy.

Ravel's early opinion on the "Affair" is unrecorded. He disliked the ardently Catholic d'Indy, founder of the Schola Cantorum, a temple of musical conservatism, but stayed silent at first, perhaps out of respect to his parents. His early letters include a couple of mildly anti-Semitic jokes, probably added to please specific correspondants, referring, for example, to the Jewish conductor Edouard Colonne as "Judas Köln." In a letter to Cipa Godebski in March 1908, Ravel wrote in jest that, although he was compared by a critic to the Jewish composer Paul Dukas, "I know very well, by gosh, that my qualities are not those of a Jew!"

In 1906 the Socialist leader Jean Jaurès called for a second retrial of Dreyfus, and Ravel, as an ardent Socialist, would no doubt have supported this measure. Dreyfus was acquitted in 1906, but his military rank and privileges were not restored, and on July 13, 1906, the military commander General Mercier refused to accept ex-Captain Dreyfus back into the army, causing violent protests. Ravel's reaction to this new miscarriage of justice survives in an exchange of letters from November 1906 with the conductor Désiré-Emile Inghelbrecht, who was "very surprised" at Ravel's "abandoning neutral territory, which almost all our mutual friends have adopted" in the Affair. He added, "Thank God you had nothing to do with that foolish incident last July," probably referring to a protest after Mercier's speech in the senate. As always, Ravel played his cards close to his chest, pointing out to Inghelbrecht that that there were "certain places" where they could no longer talk openly, and proposing a private meeting to "arrange our mutual attitudes by honest explanations."

Meanwhile, Ravel's compositional skills developed alongside his political involvement; his next work was inspired by one of the more flamboyant members of the *Apaches* group, the poet Arthur Justin Léon Leclère (1874–1966), who took what one friend called a "double-Wagnerian" pen name, Tristan Klingsor. A known homosexual and enthusiast for everything Oriental, Klingsor published a collection of poems in 1903, *Shéhérazade*, named after Rimsky-Korsakov's orchestral work, but his real knowledge of the Orient was limited to the paintings of Léon Bakst, Rimsky's compositions, and a new translation of the *1001 Nights* by the French doctor J. C. Mardrus. This had been published between 1899 and 1904 and delighted Marcel Proust, among others, for its sexual license, celebrating the beauty of boy cupbearers and casting an amused eye at pederasts who pursued them. Typically, Ravel told friends he preferred the earlier version of the *1001 Nights* by eighteenth-century translator Antoine Galland, a controlled and relatively bowdlerized version, whereas Mardrus emphasized scabrous details.

In 1903 Ravel asked Klingsor to read aloud three poems, "Asie," "La Flûte enchantée," and "L'Indifférent." He acquired the habit of hearing poetry spoken aloud from Viñes, who recited from memory works by Baudelaire, Hérédia, Gautier, Mallarmé, Jammes, and Claudel. The beginning of Klingsor's poem, "Asie, Asie, Asie" echoes "L'Azur, l'azur, l'azur!", the ending of Mallarmé's poem "Brise marine." A theme shared by Mallarmé and Klingsor is the need to break loose from civilization and escape to exotic life. In "Asie" Klingsor wrote unconsciously funny lines, "And keeping like Sindbad my old Arab pipe / from time to time between my lips"; the word *pipe* in French is a slang term for a blow job, and in his song Ravel prudently changed the pipe to "an old Arab cup" to be raised to the singer's lips. The second song, *La Flûte enchantée* [The Magic Flute], which was marked by the composer "very slowly, sweet and expressive," tells how a beloved woman in a harem enjoys kisses transmitted by a flute melody, while her master sleeps. The soft, drawn-out ending is one of the rare occasions where Ravel's music sounds like Debussy's. *L'Indifférent,* the last poem in the cycle, is a wistful love lyric to a beautiful youth in the pederastic tradition of medieval Arab poetry. From the start, some friends saw this song as a discreet avowal of Ravel's homosexuality. The critic Emile Vuillermoz, who knew Ravel as an *Apache,* wondered about the "rare ambiguity" of this song, telling of a young stranger whose eyes are as "gentle as a girl's" and who goes on his way, "slightly swaying in his feminine and weary gait." Vuillermoz asked, "Does this youth reject the invitation of a courtesan or that of a Greek philosopher?" He concluded, "When one knows about what has been called Ravel's sexual enigma, that he was also an 'indifférent,' one remains troubled by the delicate mystery floating around this little text, full of such strange resonances, and notices that in this page, the musician has unveiled one of the best-protected zones of his sensibility. He abandons his usual modesty and gives himself up to a sort of lyrical effusion, discreet but penetrating, that constitutes a confession exceptional in all his work."

Its homoerotic mood was clear from the beginning. One conductor of an early performance ironically said that he hoped a woman was indeed going to sing *L'Indifférent*. Ravel did write the cycle with a male singer in mind, although it was first performed by Jane Hatto, a soprano at the Paris Opéra. Significantly, Ravel himself later pointed to *L'Indifférent* as a leading example of emotional expression in his compositions.

The same year, Ravel set a group of Greek folksongs in his *Cinq mélodies populaires grecques*, for his friend the critic Dimitri Michel Calvocoressi. Calvo, as his friends called him, had organized a lecture about Greek song as the expression of an oppressed people, and, with a day and a half's notice, Ravel scribbled down piano accompaniments for five of the melodies chosen by Calvo. Two of these, *Quel galant m'est comparable,* and *Chanson des cueilleuses de lentisques,* wound up in the final work.

Cinq mélodies populaires grecques (1904–1906) begins with a brightly optimistic *Chanson de la mariée,* with a virginally pure vocal line, and continues with *Là-bas, vers l'église,* a song about the church of Ayio Sidcor, with a pious melody that leans toward Italian opera. A deceptively simple accompaniment has a touch of Mussorgsky in the bell-tolling bass. The third song is a wake-up call from a gallant soldier who brags about his pistols and "good, keen sword hanging at my side," narcissistically praising his own beauty. As in *Shéhérazade,* gender-bending is evident in the lyrics, which are usually performed by women singers. Critic Jeremy Sams states that Ravel "frequently prefer[s] a female voice in a male song—disguise, paradox, and personation are everything." The *Chanson des cueilleuses de lentisques* [Song of the Lentisk Gatherers] is a resigned, humble laborer's hopeless love ode to a passerby "more handsome than an angel," an inaccessible youth passionately loved; the song has echoes of maternal suffering. Even in folklore, Ravel brought complexities of gender to bear on his creativity. The last song, *Si gai,* introduces a prettily dancing melody, rather than ending with a downbeat song about hopeless love. *Cinq mélodies populaires grecques* is best when sung in Greek by a woman, like the mezzo-soprano Irma Kolassi, as it can seem twee in Calvo's French translation.

Ravel also toyed with gender in jokes to friends. Around this time, Calvo compiled an unpublished "Comical Dictionary of Music," inviting contributions from his *Apache* friends: Ravel jotted down two pages of ideas, of which only a few were printable, according to Calvo, including:

"Octave—a Roman emperor who measured eight notes from one end to the other."

"Viole—an ancient instrument considered to be a crime." (In French, *Viole* means both viol and rape.)

Calvo also left a notebook full of "more personal" memories of Ravel, penetrating beneath his friend's "dryness and aloofness," which would make fascinating reading if it ever turned up in an archive. He wrote in the *Musical Quarterly* that Ravel was "endowed with a great capacity for indifference and also contempt. . . . Behind the cutting manner, the irony, and aloofness, there lurked an even greater capacity for affection." Acquaintances like the pianist Arthur Rubinstein, who knew Ravel for decades, claimed that he always showed "complete indifference for everybody around him."

That summer, Ravel was brought by Viñes to the salon of Ida and Cyprien (Cipa) Godebski, where he rubbed elbows with Cocteau, Valéry, Gide, Larbaud, Satie, Roussel, and Bonnard. The Godebskis were understanding about an artist's needs and were generous with invitations despite their own limited resources. Ravel was a frequent guest in their country home, called La Grangette, outside Fontainbleau, where he found a peaceful working atmosphere.

In 1905, with his career rapidly advancing, he made one last try for the Prix de Rome, but the judges decided that his entry was not technically worthy to get past the first round of competition. This slap in the face of a thirty-year-old who had already produced *Jeux d'eau,* the String Quartet and *Shéhérazade* caused a public scandal, although numerous technical errors in his entry suggest that he was not putting the best of himself in these forced settings of texts and fugues. Misia Godebska Edwards (later known as Misia Sert), the half sister of Cipa Godebski, claimed to have led a campaign of protest after Ravel's rejection, attacking the Conservatoire's fusty decay. In a letter to the director of the Académie des Beaux Arts, novelist Romain Rolland said that while he had "no personal sympathy" for Ravel's art, he found Ravel's rejection "a condemnation for all time of these juries." Paris art notables agreed, and the Conservatoire director, Dubois, resigned and was replaced by Gabriel Fauré.

With Fauré as head of the Conservatoire, Ravel could have been appointed to a teaching post, but he did not want one.

Instead, he took refuge on the yacht of Misia Godebska Edwards, whose then-husband, Alfred Edwards, owned the newspaper *Le Matin.* Before he left Paris, however, Ravel finished a new work, *Introduction et Allegro,* for harp, flute, clarinet, and string quartet. After a brief introduction, the allegro is like a sketch of daybreak in *Daphnis et Chloé,* a rustling forth into life. The harp part takes a leading lyric role, as in Mozart's *Concerto for Flute and Harp,* alternating with somber strumming like a Spanish guitar. A pleasing divertimento, *Introduction et Allegro* has become one of Ravel's most popular pieces, and is also one of his smoothest and least challenging. Ravel talked of dropping this deft and elegant piece from his catalogue of published works, perhaps because it tended toward what critics saw as one of his main faults, substituting seductive grace for feeling.

On the Edwards' yacht, the revelers went to Belgium, Holland, and Germany. Ravel adapted the logo on the yacht flags, ME (for Misia Edwards), into a monogram, MR, which he used in letters and musical scores for the rest of his life. This hard-edged image had the hieroglyphic power of an ancient drawing of a dancer, solid and masculine (MR could also be read as "Monsieur").

From Germany, Ravel wrote to his fellow *Apache* Maurice Delage about factories he visited, calling them "a wonderful symphony of assembly lines, whistles, and terrific hammer blows. . . . What music there is in all this, and I surely plan to use it." Instead, a song was produced next, *Le Noël des jouets,* to a text by Ravel, depicting the glitter of Christmas gifts. Belzébuth, a sinister dog, stares at the Christ child. The presence of evil in the Garden, or in the nativity scene, is a tradition in religious iconography. For example, Hugo Wolf's song, *Auf ein altes Bild,* to a poem by Edouard Mörike, describes a painting of the Virgin and Child in which the cross is already present. Ravel's poem and song are folkloric, with mechanical livestock whose high-pitched voices bleat "Noël! Noël!" Harsh assonances, like the final "grêle bêle Noël," suggest a rattling primitivism.

In 1905 Ravel made an arrangement with the music publisher Durand, who would publish his works for the rest of his life. According to the contract, the publisher was to have the right of first refusal of Ravel's new works in exchange for a retainer fee of 12,000 francs, a modest sum. Ravel confessed to Calvo that he would have preferred half of that sum in order to feel less obliged to produce music that pleased his publisher.

Meanwhile, on Janury 6, Ricardo Viñes gave the first public performance of Ravel's new piano work, *Miroirs,* finished the preceding year. Each movement is dedicated to a member of the *Apache* group: *Noctuelles* (Léon-Paul Fargue), *Oiseaux tristes* (Ricardo Viñes), *Une barque sur l'océan* (Paul Sordes), *Alborada del gracioso* (Michel Calvocoressi), and *La Vallée des cloches* (Maurice Delage). Despite these dedications, the title *Miroirs* [Mirrors] suggests that the composer-as-narcissist was as concerned with his own reflection as with portraying friends. Ravel quoted a tag from the first act of a French translation of Shakespeare's *Julius Caesar,* where Cassius asks Brutus if he can see his own face, and Brutus replies: "No, Cassius, for the eye sees not itself/ But by reflection, from some other thing."

Noctuelles [Owlet Moths] is a forthright, communicative piece about a fluttering moth. Ravel identified with flying insects, which also appear in *L'Enfant et les sortilèges,* and during his final illness at Saint-Jean-de-Luz, he told a visiting priest, "I'm a butterfly, Padre, close the window or I might fly out." *Oiseaux tristes* offers a sense of empty space and loneliness, with resounding echoes that suggest that the sad birds in the title took refuge in a bell tower. The *Apaches* to whom Ravel first played his *Miroirs* did not appreciate *Oiseaux tristes,* comparing Ravel to a vendor holding two miserable little birds that no one wants to buy. His tone was considered a little bathetic. By contrast, *Une barque sur l'océan* has the lush buoyancy of the sea, although the composer didn't enjoy maritime crossings. He complained about the English Channel, and before his trip to America, he was nervous about rough seas.

Alborada del gracioso means Gracioso's dawn serenade. Gracioso was a character in seventeenth-century Spanish plays by Tirso da Molina and others. He was scatological, sexual, antifeminist, anti-Semitic, and a vehicle for wild, antiheroic satire. He was often a servant who parodied his master's love by talking about the laxative he had taken or by breaking wind onstage. A gross trickster with license to every obscenity, Gracioso could also be poignant, but mostly he burlesqued eroticism by declaring as identical hermaphrodites, homosexuals, and eunuchs. A number of Ravel's friends believed that, in the *Alborada,* Ravel drew a self-portrait as Gracioso, the antihero of romance, someone who looked at heterosexual love as an exterior observer or mirror-image antithesis.

Alborada, the best-known part of *Miroirs* since Ravel orchestrated it in 1918, is sprightly and raucous, with a dangerously brusque edge. Like other self-portraits in *Miroirs,* Gracioso is akin to Goya's portraits of Spanish royalty, which look so nasty that one wonders if they were intended as satire.

La Vallée des cloches, the final work in *Miroirs,* begins with high notes like Liszt's *La campanella,* in the mountainside tranquility of bell towers, after the excitement of Gracioso's dance.

Miroirs was transposed into fiction by the novelist Arnold Bennett, then living in Paris. He met Ravel at Cipa Godebski's salon, and soon after writing *The Old Wives' Tale* in 1908, he produced a new novel, *The Glimpse.* This book, generally seen as an artistic failure, was strongly influenced by Ravel's public persona and work. In the first scene of the novel, the hero, Morrice Loring, is at a concert listening to Ravel's *Miroirs.* A snob and dandy, Loring presumes that he is one of the few present who can appreciate the new music, although one day Ravel's music might be understood by the "crass multitude." Bennett shrewdly describes contemporary attitudes toward Ravel in Loring's reactions: "I exulted in the acute distinction, the aristocratic audacity, the baffling obscurity of this ruthless and soft music. I thought how fine and glorious it was to hear these sounds now for the first time heard in London. I could have cried angrily to the audience: 'Shout, for the immortal spirit of beauty has passed into another incarnation, and you before all others in this city have witnessed the advent.'"

Ravel himself would have been unable to read the book, as it was never translated into French, and Bennett's journal reflects his fluctuating opinion of Ravel. In June 1908 he noted, "Godebski and his wife, Maurice Ravel, and a nameless boy of about 20 came yesterday. . . . I reflected that I liked the company of boys of 20, and that I ought to cultivate it." During World War I, the critic Ernest Newman reproached Ravel, saying to Bennett, "No great man is ever idle." (According to many observers, Ravel wasted time in nightclubs and society gatherings.) Bennett agreed this was "very true." But after hearing an all-Ravel concert in London in 1928, Bennett was pleased to declare, "It seemed to me to be *all* good music."

At the end of 1906, Ravel made an orchestral transcription of *Une barque sur l'océan,* but withdrew it after an unsuccessful public performance in February 1907. Ever short of cash, he tried to make ends meet by tutoring small groups of students in music theory. Meanwhile, another first performance precipitated a new scandal. The setting of five poems from Jules Renard's wry collection of barnyard vignettes, *Histoires naturelles,* written the previous year, was sung by Jane Bathori at the Société Nationale on January 12. The texts are dense and prosy in their humanizing, acerbic look at animals. Ravel said that they inspired "a particular kind of musical declamation, closely related to the French language's inflections," but they also marked a break with "serious" traditions of French music.

From *Histoires naturelles* Ravel selected *Le Paon* [Peacock], *Le Grillon* [Cricket], *Le Cygne* [Swan], *Le Martin-Pecheur* [Kingfisher], and *La Pintade* [Guinea Hen]. In novels by Huysmans and poems by Robert de Montesquiou, the peacock and the swan expressed the soul of the dandy, aloof and disdainful of others, showing but never offering themselves. Ravel may have intended a self-portrait in the peacock, who cries "Léon, Léon," surely not coincidentally, the name of Ravel's beloved friend, Fargue. The piano introduction for the peacock is rollickingly jaunty and weighty enough to introduce a baby elephant. "Asian" harmonies evoke the Oriental splendor of the bird, who walks around spreading his tail after having been stood up by his fiancée.

In the second song, *Le Grillon,* a cricket weary of wandering puts his house in order. Unlike Schubert's songs, in which crickets are human companions, here the singer becomes insectified, scaled down to the insect's chores. Like Mussorgsky's *Ballet of the Unhatched Chicks,* this song celebrates the evanescent lightness of vivid little things. Ravel's friend André Suarès called him a "Spanish cricket," which raises the possibility of another self-portrait. *Histoires naturelles* may be seen as more "mirrors" in which Ravel examined himself. Unlike other barnyard humorists in music like Chabrier, Ravel created natural histories that are coolly deadpan, not overtly jolly.

Jules Renard received bad marks from most writers on Ravel for his lack of interest in the cycle, but he was at worst politely self-protective. He had no ear for music, and, like most nonmusical people, especially writers, he found concerts a waste of time. He suffered at *Pelléas et Mélisande* in 1902, as he wrote in his journal: "A somber dullness, and how not to laugh at the puerility of a husband pointing to his wife and singing, 'I attach no importance to that!' It's sung conversation. I was waiting for a rhyme that never came. . . . In music I prefer an aria that sounds to me like an aria." In 1906, when Thadée Natanson told him about Ravel's setting of *Histoires naturelles,* he impishly described Ravel as someone who made Debussy look "like a graybeard." Renard was instantly wary of the project. When Natanson asked, "What effect does the idea have on you?" Renard replied, "None." Natanson countered, "Come on, you're touched." "Nope." "What should I tell [Ravel] from you?" "Whatever you want. Tell him thanks."

Renard did not forbid the settings, he just didn't want to have to hear them. But Ravel insisted that he come to a performance.

The impoverished Renard was suspicious of Ravel's dandyish appearance and assumed the young composer was rich. Finally, he sent his wife and daughter to the premiere and avoided witnessing a major scandal. The audience laughed at the line "Not a bite all evening" in *Le Martin-Pecheur*, taking the fisherman's complaint for that of an unsuccessful streetwalker, a common music-hall theme. Some critics were outraged by Ravel's "unmusical" setting, and Claude Debussy responded irritably to a copy of *Histoires naturelles* sent by his publisher, Durand: "It's excessively curious, artificial and chimerical like a witch's house." Debussy saw Ravel as a "trickster, or better, as a fakir-caster of spells, who can make flowers leap up around a chair." He saw the magical inspiration of Ravel's art as a flaw: "A trick is always premeditated and can only astonish once."

In February 1907, Debussy wrote to Louis Laloy, who had praised *Histoires naturelles*, complaining about the "deliberate Americanism" of the work, perhaps a reference to its wry, music-hall aspects. Nevertheless, the song cycle caught on, and Diaghilev considered fitting a ballet to it in Lausanne, but the project did not work out.

Ravel's notoriety as a composer was growing, but not his renown as a teacher. In February 1906, a small group of students fired Ravel as their teacher because he was often late for class. Ravel's letter about this "insolent" decision reveals his astonishment and upset.

After *Histoires naturelles* came three more songs, *Vocalise— Etude en forme d'habanera; Les Grands Vents venus d'outremer*, to a poem by Henri de Régnier; and *Sur l'herbe*, to a poem by Paul Verlaine. *Sur l'herbe* is a poetic monologue by a wayward abbot about eighteenth-century debauchery. Verlaine's poem involves giddy compliments that border on camp. This piece hearkened back to the spoofs and jokes of the *Apaches,* whose own *abbé,* curly-locked Léonce Petit, looked like a languid Persian prince. Petit wound up as chaplain of the Opéra, a high-society appointment, in which he was responsible for the eternal souls of ballet dancers and tenors.

The *Vocalise—Etude en forme d'habanera,* written for a publisher of an album of vocalises, is flamenco peppered with coloratura, with something of the vocal pyrotechnics of Donizetti's *Lucia.* Like the *Menuet antique,* the *Vocalise en forme d'habanera* mixed two genres, with a certain degree of camp sensibility. *Les Grands Vents venus d'outre-mer* is a song about "bitter adolescents who go to sea." Yet Ravel was as unlikely to break away to exotic climes as Marcel Proust. Both were attached to their mothers' apron strings.

Certain forms of exotic music always attracted him, however. Since childhood, when he played Russian music with Ricardo Viñes, Ravel had always been drawn to Slavic melodies. In 1907 the impresario Sergey Diaghilev presented a festival of Russian music in Paris, in which Rimsky-Korsakov and Glazunov conducted their music and Chaliapin sang songs by Mussorgsky. The five concerts, performed at the Opéra between May 16 and 30, made a dazzling display of noteworthy composers, from Glinka to Scriabin. At this time Ravel met Diaghilev. His close friend Calvo was an advisor for the festival, which only made a middling success. But it was an epochal event for Ravel. The next year Diaghilev returned to the Paris Opéra with Chaliapin in the title role of Mussorgsky's *Boris Godunov.*

About this time, the health of Ravel's father began to fail. Joseph Ravel suffered from depression and mental lassitude. In November, Ravel wrote to Ida Godebska that his father's "mental capacity is at its lowest: He mixes everything up, and sometimes doesn't know where he is anymore." It was one of Joseph's dreams to see his son's work in the theater, and Ravel put aside a long-term project, *The Sunken Bell*, to work on a short comic opera, *L'Heure espagnole*. This was an odd choice for an homage to a dying father, since the libretto by Franc-Nohain is a rambunctious ode to phallic potency.

Ravel's preoccupation with Spain continued later in 1907 with *Rapsodie espagnole*, originally written for piano four hands but orchestrated in the following February. The premiere was conducted in March by Edouard Colonne at his Concerts Colonne. The piece has four movements, of which the third is the *Habanera* that originally appeared as the first movement of *Sites auriculaires*. The other three are *Prelude à la nuit*, *Malagueña*, and *Feria*. It employs a large orchestra, including a sarrusophone (a French brass bassoon), a big percussion section, a celesta, and two harps. With an orchestral surge of joy, the lunar prelude describes the moment when night arrives. In *Malagueña*, wild castanets and drum alternate inexorably. In the score of the *Habanera* movement, Ravel added the date of the piano version, 1895, to establish his precedence over Debussy, who had written no Spanish music at that time. (Later critics would tax Ravel with imitating Debussy.) *Feria* is like music heard from a passing ocean liner, when suddenly the music swerves closer to the listener. The violins make a feline sound, and at the first performance, someone called from the gallery, "Where's the cat?" In January 1910, a

London Telegraph reviewer agreed: "The first violins, literally mewing like a rather deep-voiced tom cat, brought laughs from the audience." Languid passages for cellos and double basses sound like the exhausted mounts of Don Quixote and Sancho Panza, plodding along after a defeat. *Rapsodie espagnole* is a familiar orchestral showpiece that has not lost its essential strangeness. Playing with picturesque elements, Ravel never abandons experimentation, using glissandi to sometimes alarming effect.

In an article in the July 1907 edition of *Censeur politique et littéraire,* Ravel's friend Georges Jean-Aubry praised him as the "enfant terrible of current French music." No one else, according to Jean-Aubry, "sparks such fury in the musical milieu or prevents musical academicians from sleeping." But Manuel de Falla rejected the image of Ravel as an enfant terrible, stating that he was instead an *enfant prodige* [child prodigy] "whose miraculously cultivated mind performs sorceries by means of his art."

A new international friendship was forged at the end of 1907, when Ravel was introduced to Ralph Vaughan Williams, who although three years older than Ravel, had asked him for composition lessons. Vaughan Williams, mountainous and bovine-looking even when young, refused the first assignment to write a Mozartian "little minuet." He later recalled an evening with Ravel and a publisher friend, who suggested that they "go see some jolly tarts." They trooped off to a bordello where the whores were as ugly as in Toulouse-Lautrec paintings, "guaranteed not to tempt any young man to lose his virtue." The friends probably just sat, smoked, had a drink, and conversed with the "jolly tarts." A turn-of-the-century Paris whorehouse was a men's club where buying sex was one activity, but not the only one. Manuel Rosenthal later noted that Ravel was on speaking terms with whores in a Paris bistro and concluded that Ravel had "gone over to the prostitutes," just as Inghelbrecht told the biographer H. H. Stuckenschmidt that Ravel had "occasional encounters with prostitutes," and Marguerite Long wrote about his meeting an occasional "sidewalk Venus." Whatever his real relations with women prostitutes, the young Ravel still found marriage and sex incompatible. "Love never rises above licentiousness," he would later say, in response to Long's urgings that he get married and start a family.

CHAPTER THREE

To Daphnis and After

1908–1913

By 1908 Ravel was a noted figure on the Paris music scene. The 42-year-old Jean Sibelius traveled to Paris that year, staying at the home of the Scandinavian composer Emil Sjögren, and was excited when Michel Calvocoressi came over to visit, hoping that Calvo might introduce him to Ravel. Instead, the evening was spent listening to "a second-rate American singer, Minnie Tracey," and Sibelius walked home fuming, "Is it to suffer this sort of thing that one comes to Paris?"

Ravel's position was strong enough to allow him to fight injustices. The French composer Antoine Mariotte wrote an opera called *Salomé* based, like Richard Strauss's opera from the same year, on Oscar Wilde's play. Strauss's publisher tried to have it banned, and Ravel, though he disliked the Schola Cantorum music Mariotte produced, wrote an open letter of protest. Strauss's publisher withdrew their objections.

By this time Ravel had already started—and postponed—work on an opera project of his own, based on the German author Gerhart Hauptmann's verse play *The Sunken Bell,* in an abridged French translation by A. Ferdinand Hérold. Chock-full of elves and nymphs, this fairy story would never be completed, although Ravel reused some of the sketches for it in *L'Enfant et les sortilèges.* Hauptmann's verse play, dismissed today for its clumsy prosody, is about mermaids, mermen, and a malicious forest satyr, "an oversexed, pipe-smoking forest sprite." A bell, hauled to a mountain chapel, falls into a lake as punishment for the creative impotence of the play's hero. Ravel may have identified with the smoking satyr-sprite, but the heavy-handed goings-on were better suited to Ottorino Respighi, who some years later wrote a popular opera, *La Campana sommersa,* based on the same play.

About his personal life Ravel was still guarded, although he wrote lightly on sexual subjects to Ida Godebska. Around June 1908 he informed Ida that he had witnessed a meeting between her husband, Cipa, and the Italian poet Ricciotto Canudo, a bisexual propagandist for the arts in Italy and France, who worked on projects with Blaise Cendrars, Pablo Picasso, Jacob Epstein, Paul Claudel, and the film director Abel Gance. Canudo had been invited to the Godebskis' country home, and he responded to something Cipa had said by saying, "Certainly, old girl." Ravel joked that the new male friends might soon be seen on the "Mallarmé bench," suitable for "the breaking up of love affairs," a reference to a bench on the neighboring property of the Mallarmé family. With Ida, Ravel felt comfortable making pointed comments about homosexuality. In a letter in June 1908, he noted that a new play, *Le Monsieur aux chrysanthèmes,* about a homosexual love triangle, had been described by poet and critic Catulle Mendès as putting onstage "the stupidest and most repugnant of vices." Ravel's dry comment "The old guard is still virtuous" was an ironic observation on Mendès's own varied sex life.

When the director of the Opéra Comique refused to stage *L'Heure espagnole* because of its lewd subject, Ravel told Ida in a letter of February 1908 that he realized the "least innocent transgression of Carmen, Manon, Khrysis, and Queen Fiamette was to poke their fingers too often up their noses," a metaphor for heterosexual intercourse. *L'Heure espagnole* is a transcendent farce full of one-of-the-boys racy jokes. Its hurried production may have been intended as a sign to his failing father that he was capable of heterosexual interests. Joseph Ravel probably wondered about the *Apaches,* some of them publicly known homosexuals. *L'Heure espagnole* possibly reassured his father but was no more sincere than Ravel thought any art should be. The falseness of his heterosexual posturing would have made it all the more artistically viable according to his aesthetic.

L'Heure espagnole contains a French ideal of quicksilver speed and wit. It is an endless delight to listen to, just as it is hard to perform, because the orchestral jokes are so numerous. Mocking mating rituals, Ravel offered a comic version of Leonardo da Vinci's anatomical drawing of a couple having sexual intercourse.

Franc-Nohain's libretto combined grievously funny puns and sexual anarchy, but the music, so utterly refined and masterful, transcends the genre of French sex farce. Its rampant musical invention transforms the libretto's preoccupations with phallic triumph and heavy jokes about love and death.

The first scene opens with three metronomes ticking at differ-ent speeds at a clockmaker's shop. Ravel specified that the metronomes should be set at 40, 100, and 232, the last being faster than the standard metronome can function, while the orchestra is playing at a basic tempo of 72, or a military "slow march." Torquemada, a cuckolded watchmaker, receives a visit from the muleteer Ramiro, who claims that his watch was damaged when his uncle was gored by a bull (here the orchestra makes a bull-like sound). Torquemada's faithless wife, Concepcion, enters to a little mock-romantic melody in the tradition of Italian opera. She waits impatiently for her husband to leave on his weekly round to wind the town's clocks. This is when she regularly meets her lover, a precious hour of freedom which is now threatened by the presence of Ramiro.

To get rid of him, Concepcion asks the muleteer to move one of two heavy grandfather clocks up to her bedroom. In an Alice-in-Wonderland shrinking of what is big to what is little, the mule-teer insists that the clocks are merely "a straw, a nut kernel, etc." As he disappears upstairs, Concepcion's lover, Gonzalve, wan-ders in, warbling in the best tenor style, but because the lovers are not alone in the house, he is promptly asked to hide in a large grandfather clock. The muleteer Ramiro, none the wiser, is asked to carry the suddenly quite heavy clock up to Concepcion's bed-room, and he performs the task brilliantly. However, more clock stuffing is in order when another suitor, a voluminous banker named Don Inigo Gomez, arrives on the scene and is also obliged to hide inside a clock. Once again Ramiro is asked to bear the burden upstairs, but Concepcion concludes that her two suitors are each unsatisfactory in their own way: the poet is too poetic and the banker too absurd. Her eye lights upon Ramiro, who has performed such feats of strength with good cheer, and she decides to take him as her new lover. The two exit to her bedroom, and Torquemada the clockmaker returns home, finding the two rejected swains in their clocks, which he promptly sells to them. Concepcion returns with her muleteer, but her husband remains joyful about his unexpected sales, and the opera concludes with a comic quintet that states the moral, "A moment arrives in the diversions of love when the muleteer has his turn!"

There was some gap of understanding between composer and librettist, a successful farceur but no refined artist. Franc-Nohain had only one reply when Ravel played him the piano version of *L'Heure espagnole*—he pointed to his pocket watch and said, "Fifty-six minutes." Perhaps for the librettist, it was a mechanical sex farce, where the swinging of pendulums echo the in-and-out of sexual intercourse. Ravel himself described *L'Heure espagnole* as "a Molièresque parody of life in a Spanish setting; it must be taken as nonchalantly as one eats a bonbon." Molière's influence is clear in the way the libretto is divided into "scenes" for one or two characters, as in seventeenth-century plays. The distancing of the erotic comedy transformed it into art. The opera's title, usually translated as The Spanish Hour, could also be rendered as Spanish Time, or What Time It Is in Spain, a light-hearted reference to customs abroad. Although Concepcion's search for lovers may seem mechanical on paper, onstage there was charm and seduction when she was played by beautiful singing actresses like Lucrezia Bori, Conchita Supervia, Fanny Heldy, and Denise Duval. Then, Concepcion's youthful sparkle recalls the élan of Rosina in Rossini's *Barber of Seville*.

There are serious themes in all this: "Our time is measured piti-lessly," as Concepcion observes. The clock is a memento mori, an urging on to physical pleasures, because life is short. When Gon-zalves hides in the second clock, to be carried into her bedroom in a parody of the Trojan Horse, he declares that his love is "stronger than death." Concepcion remarks that "clocks have ears," and the orchestra's wind instruments tick with winking complicity. Again and again, the orchestra comments on the stage action, as in burlesque theaters where a drummer follows a dancer's bumps and grinds. Ravel was inspired by the immediacy and comic freshness of the popular theater. High art is also paro-died. To evoke the seasick effect of being lurched around inside a clock, Ravel employs a harp as did Debussy in *La Mer*.

All of this flies by the listener in condensed form. Cocking a snoot at operatic conventions, Ravel's jokes are too witty to be called camp. He brilliantly altered kitsch to serve his own means, rather than reveling in it for its own sake.

Once *L'Heure espagnole* was finished, its staging was delayed, even after the piano-vocal score was published in 1908. At first it was scheduled to be performed on a double bill with Richard Strauss's romantic opera *Feuersnot,* but fortunately this plan was altered. The love scene from *Feuersnot* had displeased Colette when she heard it in March 1903, as music critic for *Gil Blas:* "My ears are still going bzi, bzi ! That's a love scene? *Wellll,* if my ecstasy was that tumultuous, I'd like to see what my downstairs neighbors would say."

Ravel's own tumult was not staged until 1911, after the inter-vention of Madame Jean Cruppi, the wife of a French govern-ment minister, who pressured Albert Carré to put the work on.

Ravel dedicated the opera to her, as well as his song, *Le Noël des jouets*. Before the performance he felt obliged to write an open letter to *Le Figaro* explaining his intentions, in order to ward off the kind of scandal that had greeted *Histoires naturelles*. He stated that he wished to revive the "principle" of Italian opera buffa, but "only the principle" and that in fact his opera's "only direct ancestor" was *The Marriage* by Mussorgsky, after a play by Gogol.

When the opera was staged on a double bill with Massenet's French Revolution opera, *Thérèse*, one critic called the libretto a "mildly pornographic vaudeville." Franc-Nohain replied that his play had been printed in the *Revue de Paris* and performed over a hundred times at the Théâtre de l'Odéon. On opening night, Ravel was mainly concerned because the *beau monde* wore stylish blue evening clothes, while he, whose tailor had not managed to finish his new blue suit in time, was in old-fashioned black evening wear.

L'Heure espagnole was only performed a few times, then removed from the repertoire until after World War I, when it began to be performed outside France. Its erotic elements did not appeal to one influential Italian critic, Guido Pannain, who wrote: "The sex-ridden woman, who weeps tears of sheer lust for a brawny navvy's arms, is no character for Ravel's music—that subtle mosaic of sound—to interpret."

Between May and September 1908, Ravel worked on *Gaspard de la Nuit,* piano pieces inspired by the poems of the nineteenth-century writer Aloysius Bertrand, a magical work in three sections, *Ondine, Le Gibet,* [The Gallows], and *Scarbo*. Its first performance was by Ricardo Viñes in January 1909.

In *Ondine,* a water nymph appears in sparkling foam amid a suave melodic line. Little bursts of melodic energy give the impression of a cup running over. *Le Gibet* is a portrait of the gallows. Soothingly deep chords open this picture of death, and hanging starts to seem like an inevitable end. The final movement, *Scarbo,* named after a goblin, is Mussorgskian in its ominous chords, bursting into virtuosic runs to depict a demonic rampage. Like a Morse code operator gone mad, the pianist raps out Asian-sounding groups of high notes. After a great, malignant, hopping dance, there are low echoing notes, and slowly the whirling returns in the best horror-film style: "He's baaaaack!" The classical tradition of da capo offers an encore within the piece itself. The pianist goes up and down in demented reiteration as Scarbo exults in his own wickedness. The lushness of the end is like the dense final aria in Richard Strauss's *Salomé,* celebrating the erotic triumph of malignancy. "I have been evil," Scarbo crows, but unlike Salomé, crushed to death by Herod's soldiers after her aria, he is applauded by the audience after his star turn. In a letter to Ida Godebska in July 1908, Ravel reported that *Gaspard* had been "the devil to finish, which is logical since He was the author."

In 1908, interested as ever in poets, Ravel visited Paul Valéry, whom he told that "one of his deepest impressions" had been reading that writer's "Soirée avec M. Teste." This was an abstract portrait of a man obsessed with his feelings and detached from his own life. Ravel must have agreed with Mr. Teste's advice about the value of creative solitude: "Give yourself wholly to your best moment, to your finest memory. . . . The thing that is really important to oneself—I mean the one in us who is in essence unique and alone—is just that which makes him feel that he is alone." In his *Cahiers*, Valéry recalled trying to explain during chats with Ravel his idea of bringing "wastelands" like poetry and philosophy into harmony with the modern scientific mind. "Ravel didn't understand anything I was saying," he commented, yet he paid tribute in a notebook reference to "the pure musician (Bach-Ravel)" and sketched a picture of Ravel's back while he played his *Sonatine* and *Alborada del gracioso*.

In October of this same year, 1908, Joseph Ravel died after a long wasting illness. The family moved from Levallois-Perret to a more central flat on the avenue Carnot in Paris' seventeenth arrondissement. Living in this apartment during World War I, Maurice would often disappear from the house in the afternoon, only to return at eleven P.M. or later. Asked where he had been and what he had done, he would only reply that he couldn't remember. Edouard later saw this as early evidence of the neurological malady that plagued Maurice's final years, but it merely may have been an escape from the family circle, to lead a life of his own. Madame Bonnet, a family friend, said that Ravel's mother tolerated his nocturnal ways, but "no other woman could have lived with Maurice. His habits were too irregular. . . . He got up late and often worked all day in his pyjamas. At seven, when she was ready to serve dinner, he would rush out 'for a walk' and return only at midnight."

He was equally evasive with friends. At a party in the home of Madame de Saint-Marceaux, Ravel announced, "I prefer a lovely locomotive to a lovely woman! In fact, my only mistress is music." Not all salon-goers appreciated hearing him perform, as

Arnold Bennett noted in May 1914 about an evening party where Ravel and Alfredo Casella played the piano. A French guest said, "The music stopped just before it got boring, and then there was a really good buffet." Bennett commented drily, "All countries are alike."

In April 1909 Ravel made his first trip to London for a concert of his works, which included the *Sonatine,* the Greek folk melodies, and *Histoires naturelles.* He stayed with Ralph Vaughan Williams and astonished his host by relishing steak and kidney pudding washed down with stout, at a Waterloo Station restaurant. Ravel asked Vaughan Williams to be taken to "Vallasse," which the Englishman correctly guessed meant the Wallace Collection.

After his father's death, Ravel was shocked into a period of musical silence, with the exception of a brief *Menuet sur le nom de Haydn,* written in response to a commission from the editor of the *Revue musicale de la S.I.M.,* who also asked for musical homages on the centenary of Haydn's death from Debussy, Paul Dukas, Reynaldo Hahn, Vincent d'Indy, and Charles-Marie Widor. For Ravel, an homage to Haydn had clear paternal parallels, as the eighteenth-century composer was called Papa and was an artistic ancestor of Ravel. He found inspiration in the witty minuets of Haydn, as well as those of Cimarosa and Couperin, in neoclassic works like the *Sonatine,* Quartet, and *D'Anne jouant de l'espinette.* The *Menuet sur le nom de Haydn* offers gently consoling musical phrasing, a palpably affectionate, fatherly caress that recalls the photo of Joseph Ravel embracing his two sons. The slight piece does not sound like Haydn, but it evokes a lost time of tender emotions.

In 1909 the great impresario Sergey Diaghilev brought his Ballets Russes company to Paris. The operas he presented in France were serious musical statements, but the first series of ballets he imported had undistinguished scores, like Nikolay Tchérepnine's musty *Le Pavillon d'Armide,* and a clunky reorchestration of Chopin, *Les Sylphides.* Dancers like Vaslav Nijinsky, Tamara Karsavina, and Anna Pavlova distracted audiences from the meager music. But Diaghilev was soon convinced of the need for fresh new scores like Stravinsky's *L'Oiseau de feu* [Firebird] and *Pétrouchka.* Diaghilev, who was violently in love with Nijinsky, decided after a triumphant Paris season to commission new ballets from Stravinsky, Ravel, and Falla, although he had no money to pay for them.

Diaghilev commissioned *Daphnis et Chloé* from Ravel and a ballet to be called *Masques et Bergamasques* from Debussy. But Debussy was highly suspicious of Diaghilev, accusing him privately to friends of "chicanery" and quoting a maxim supposedly from Kipling, "A Russian is a charming person until he puts on his shirt." Not surprisingly, Debussy never wrote the requested ballet, although his *L'Après-midi d'un faune,* not intially intended as a ballet, became one of Nijinsky's most famous vehicles. Diaghilev also initiated talks about a ballet to be done by Cocteau and Reynaldo Hahn, which became *Le Dieu bleu,* an Indian fantasy. Thanks to an idea from Calvo, Diaghilev also asked for a ballet from Gabriel Fauré, who was too busy with his opera *Pénélope* to comply. Michel Fokine was choreographer for the planned *Daphnis et Chloé,* whose story came from a Greek tale by Longus, with music by Ravel. Fokine had hoped to stage a Daphnis ballet since

1904, and had many ideas on the subject, which were not always shared by Diaghilev and Ravel.

Ravel was present at the May 1909 Paris premiere of the Ballets Russes, along with notables like Pierre Lalo, Gabriel Fauré, and Camille Saint-Saëns. That night Nijinsky danced *Le Pavillon d'Armide* by Tchérepnine, and the dancer's long leaps impressed Ravel, who later included silences in *Daphnis* to accommodate Nijinsky-sized jumps. The following year, Diaghilev decided that he needed a Russian ballet for the May season at the Paris Opéra and the Drury Lane Theatre in London, and Stravinsky composed *L'Oiseau de feu* to fit the bill, although he complained that the ballet commission "demanded descriptive music of a kind I did not want to write." At the end of 1910, Stravinsky began writing another immortal ballet for Diaghilev's Ballets Russes, *Pétrouchka*, which became one of Nijinsky's last great roles.

The same year, Ravel broke with the Société Nationale de Musique, after the group refused to perform a work by one of his students and friends, Maurice Delage. Ravel, Fauré, Charles Koechlin, and a number of other, more free-thinking composers banded together to form the Société Musicale Indépendante to sponsor their own adventurous concerts. For the first SMI concert on April 20, 1910, Ravel wrote a work for two pianists, *Ma Mère l'Oye* [Mother Goose].

Ma Mère l'Oye, later orchestrated as a ballet, was first intended to be performed by Jean and Mimie Godebski, his friends' two children. However, Mimie froze at the idea of performing a new work in public, and so the premiere was entrusted to two students at the Conservatoire, Jeanne Leleu, eleven years old, and Geneviève Durony, fourteen. Ravel wrote to Jeanne Leleu after the performance, thanking her for her "childlike" performance, thus thanking a child for being childlike. In Ravel's aesthetic, seeming was as interesting as being, and being a child was not the same as appearing like one in front of an audience. Not everyone agreed. After the premiere, the critic Gaston Carraud called Jeanne Leleu and Geneviève Durony "péronelles," silly half-witted girls.

The two-piano version of *Ma Mère l'Oye* is divided into five sections: *Pavane de la Belle au Bois Dormant; Petit Poucet; Laideronnette, Impératrice des Pagodes: Entretiens de la Belle et de la Bête;* and *Le Jardin féerique.* The stories were drawn from the fairy tales by the authors Charles Perrault, Madame d'Aulnoy, and Madame Leprince de Beaumont.

The opening piece, *Pavane de la Belle au Bois Dormant* [Sleeping Beauty's Pavane], portrays a world of childhood enchantment. A recurring theme is the metamorphosis of adult love; the second section, *Petit Poucet* [Tom Thumb], expresses inner anxiety, as a possible self-portrait of Ravel, the miniature man. The title of the third section, *Laideronette, Impératrice des Pagodes* [Laideronnette, Empress of the Pagodes], refers to the Asian musical instrument, pagodes, rather than pagoda buildings. Laideronette comes from a tale by Marie d'Aulnoy, "Serpentin vert," in which a princess is cursed by a wicked fairy to a life of ugliness, until she meets a large green snake whom she marries. At once she becomes beautiful, and the snake turns into a handsome prince. Embracing ugliness, and the metamorphosis of ugliness into beauty, are themes in the fourth section, *Entretiens et la Belle et la Bête* [Conversations between Beauty and the Beast]. Here Ravel quotes excerpts from the fairy tale:

"When I think how good-hearted you are, you do not seem to me so ugly."

"Oh, lady! Yes, I have a kind heart, but I am a monster."

"There are many men more monstrous than you."

"If I had wit, I would invent a fine compliment to thank you, but I am only a beast."

The exchange is informed with a poignant sense of sexual unattractiveness. The Beast's ugliness requires a major metamorphosis in order to be acceptable to Beauty.

Fairy tales can often conceal adult emotions in childlike contexts. The nineteenth-century gay author Hans Christian Andersen was a key modern developer of the genre, expressing a personal sense of unattractiveness in stories like "The Ugly Duckling." Using seventeenth- and eighteenth-century fairy tales, Ravel still followed in the mid-Victorian tradition of Andersen and Grimm, treating romantic themes through fairy stories. Indeed, *Ma Mère l'Oye* may be grouped with the ballet *Adélaïde, ou le langage des fleurs* as a yearning for an obsolete rhetoric of love, a code language of desire. For sexual love to be possible, a magical changing of bodies is necessary: Beasts must become men, or vice versa.

The French critic Roland Barthes perceived the sexual complexity of Ravel's work and would later use *Ma Mère l'Oye* as a key text in his book *Fragments d'un discours amoureux*, which dissects a gay romance. Barthes discussed *Les Entretiens de la Belle et de la Bête*, alongside Goethe's *Werther*. As a "beast"-like older lover of a handsome young man, Barthes felt at home with Ravel's allegory, and in the music he heard that although the Beast was a prisoner of his own ugliness, he eventually managed to conquer Beauty. An artful glissando represents the change of Beast into Prince Charming. The pieces ends with *Le Jardin féerique,* or enchanted garden, which reaches a climax that the pianist Alfred Cortot said was influenced by Fauré. Its sober chords, marked "slow and with gravity," are of a rare lyric beauty.

When he orchestrated the work as a ballet in 1911, a prelude, *Danse du rouet* [Dance of the Spinning Wheel], was added along with some varied interludes to link the scenes. The new prelude, marked "very slowly," is mysteriously disturbing. The *Danse du rouet* that follows evokes the tale of Princess Florine, who is stuck by an old woman's spinning wheel and drops off into a deep sleep. This is a natural introduction to the *Pavane de la Belle au Bois Dormant* that follows, in which the old woman is revealed to be a good fairy. Next, *Entretiens de la Belle et la Bête* is shuffled to an earlier position than in the piano suite, which makes the love dialogue more prominent. The orchestral *Ma Mère l'Oye* seems especially defined by the theme of enchantment, which makes impossible love a reality. The composer's genius as orchestrator shines brightly in the next two movements, *Petit Poucet,* with violins and flutes that represent birdcalls, and *Laideronnette, Impératrice des Pagodes,* with breathtakingly rich combinations of cymbals, harp, celesta, and xylophone and passionate strings. The finale, *Le Jardin féerique* builds up to a majestic conclusion for the whole orchestra, and what seemed unplayable on one piano suddenly finds its true scale.

In September 1916 Diaghilev showed interest in staging *Ma Mère l'Oye,* but Ravel had his publisher Durand discourage the project, as he explained in a letter to Ida Godebska: "*Ma Mère l'Oye* at the Ballets Russes! Terpsichore preserve me! The Russian dancers are fearsome soldiers—nothing can resist their pointes. . . . The works they attack shine with exceptional brilliance, the brilliance of a fire. . . . I absolutely don't want *Ma Mère l'Oye* to serve as pretext for a Croatian divertimento, and prefer that this little fantasy have a more modest destiny, more respectful, less ephemeral, rather than to see it aflame in such asiatic sumptuousness."

In 1910 Ravel orchestrated *Pavane pour une infante défunte*, originally written for piano in 1899, and entered a folk-song competition organized by a Moscow group, the *Maison du Lied*, founded by a Russian singer, Marie Olénine d'Alheim, and her husband, Pierre. The society, started in 1908, invited composers to arrange folk songs with piano accompaniments. Ravel made seven settings from as many countries and won prizes for songs from Spain, France, Italy, and in the Hebrew language. He also set a Scots melody, and two others which have been lost, in Russian and Flemish. Marie Olénine d'Alheim was also noted for singing Mussorgsky's songs, and Ravel learned from her, and Chaliapin, about the neglected Russian composer. Of the *Quatres Chants Populaires* published in 1910, *Chanson hébraïque* offers sweeter harmonies than authentic synagogue music, closer to *Boris Godunov* than to Hebrew liturgy. *Chanson française* is light and transparent, while *Chanson italienne* has plenty of Neapolitan sobs, yet looks back to the majesty of old arias like *Amarilli mia bella*. *Chanson espagnole* picks up the tempo with a dance rhythm.

Ravel's musical activities were slight in 1910, but he was busy with political activities close to his heart. That year, according to

Calvo, he became an activist for the only time in his life. Defending an accused murderer, Jean-Jacques Liabeuf, Ravel allied himself with the French anarchist movement, led by Victor Serge, among others. The anarchist ideal attracted many French people as a political and social system where an individual could develop according to his natural rights and abandon traditional moral standards of a government-as-parent.

Liabeuf was a handsome young mustachioed former shoemaker's helper, jailed on a trumped-up charge of pimping. As an *Apache,* Liabeuf claimed that the vice squad cops had set him up. When he was freed, he stalked his shabby quarter, wearing over his biceps and forearms leather bands with long thin spikes. He said he had read about this weapon in a British penny thriller. When he saw the vice cops who had arrested him, Liabeuf killed one of them. He was charged with murder, and pimping for two whores from les Halles quarter. The two women denied that Liabeuf was their pimp, and a socialist journalist, Gustave Hervé, wrote in the newspaper *La Guerre sociale,* that Liabeuf "did not lack a certain beauty and grandeur" and was "anything you like, but not a pimp." Hervé asserted that the young man had given a "fine example" of vengeance for victims of police brutality, and for this statement the journalist was thrown into prison for four years.

At public demonstrations, people shouted, "Avenge Liabeuf!" The Socialist leader Jean Jaurès spoke on Liabeuf's behalf, but the young man was sentenced to death. In the days before Liabeuf's execution, Ravel and other activists hurriedly gathered signatures on petitions for clemency addressed to French president Fallières. Ravel's defense of Liabeuf was a fight against death and the hated Paris vice squad, the terror of gay men as well as heterosexuals, whose frequent arrests were widely publicized in the popular press.

Five thousand Parisians signed the petition, including Anatole France, but the prisoner was guillotined on schedule, and Ravel went home to grieve silently. Calvo recalled, "After Liabeuf's execution, Ravel was so upset that for a few days he shut himself up in his home, refusing to see anybody." On the day Liabeuf was guillotined, there were violent riots involving thirty thousand demonstrators, hundreds of whom were injured in fights with police. In the cemetery of Ivry, where he was buried, a wreath was placed, ironically dedicated "To Liabeuf, victim of the vice squad apaches."

On July 8, 1910, a week after the execution, Ravel wrote to his friend Inghelbrecht using black-bordered stationery left over from his father's death a couple of years before. Using the paper meant to mourn his father as sign of deep loss over the death of an accused pimp is a twist that might have been appreciated by Proust, who gave his own deceased parents' furniture to decorate a Parisian male bordello.

After this struggle, Ravel never again entered the political forum, although he would defiantly tell friends, "I support no party; I'm an anarchist." He explained in a letter to Ida Godebska that he was "not a moderate nor a radical socialist, nor above all, a journalist— and my anarchical simplicity is limited to applauding the little and big infamies of all the [political] parties." A month after Liabeuf's death, he wrote again to Ida, referring to a duel challenge about which little is known. He met with a Mr. Chazinski, apparently a second, "who seems to share my opinions on dueling. Finally, we decided to postpone it all until September."

Returning to work, he toiled on the *Daphnis et Chloé* commission, too slowly for Diaghilev's taste. In May 1910, Ravel wrote to Calvo, asking questions about things Russian and Greek (both specialities of Calvo's): "Still about Ganymede's compatriot, I cannot fucking remember (neurasthenia) the name of Pan's pipe (flute)." The answer was Syrinx, but the reference to Daphnis as "Ganymede's compatriot" was a typically wry tease. Ganymede was synonymous with "pederastic lover," and the sexual relationship between Nijinsky, who would dance the role, and Diaghilev was notorious. What is more, having read Longus's story in French translation, Ravel knew it contained an all-too-relevant gay episode in which Daphnis is wooed by a grotesque satyr who is "all belly and what was below," a character not retained for the ballet.

The eight waltzes in *Valses Nobles et Sentimentales* (1911, orchestrated in 1912) often vary greatly from the standard waltz form. The first two are a little jarring, with nerves on edge, which then subside into sad regret. Although Ravel named Schubert as his immediate inspiration, the layering of neurotic emotion on dance movements makes psychologically complex mood-pictures that are closer to Schumann. The worlds of E.T.A. Hoffmann and Paganini seem to be the background here, as in Schumann's piano works. Yet Ravel rejected Schumann, complaining that "just because he was a genius" he could "poison the general musical taste with his sickening sentimentality."

The epilogue, beginning like Schumann's *Prophet Bird,* ends in mystery and interrogation. *Valses nobles et sentimentales* asks more oblique questions than it answers, and its emotional complexity is Jamesian in breadth of cultural reference.

Valses nobles et sentimentales was first performed at a concert of the SMI in May 1911; the program was presented anonymously, and the audience was asked to identify the composers, who ranged from Inghelbrecht to Couperin. Although a "slight majority" correctly identified Ravel, some listeners thought the *Valses nobles et sentimentales* were by Satie or Kodály, choices that have been scorned by writers with the advantage of hindsight.

In 1912 Ravel's orchestral versions of *Ma Mère l'Oye* and *Valses nobles et sentimentales* were staged as ballets. He wrote scenarios with detailed action for both, the only time he was involved so closely with ballet action. *Valses nobles et sentimentales* became *Adélaïde, ou le langage des fleurs,* fashioned for the ballerina Natalie Trouhanova. She was no great dancer but was the mistress of an important composer, Paul Dukas. The language of flowers is a tradition dating back to Renaissance Italy, revived in books during early Victorian times, first in France, then in England. The idea originated in travelers' tales about oriental courtship in Turkish harems. By combining certain flowers into bouquets, phrases like "I have faith in you, but you have hurt me" could be communicated. Books about the largely mythical significance of flowers were popular with ladies around 1820, Ravel's favorite era, and by following the craze for flower meanings, he hearkened back to the time of his grandparents' courtship. Like fairy tales, flowers offered an erotic code, a secret way of communicating desire that dared not speak its name otherwise. At an ironic, critical remove from the waltz form, as he would later be with *La Valse,* the composer was offering a commentary on social communication between the sexes. Heterosexual romance was a foreign country for Ravel, who needed a

Baedecker at hand in order to understand it. His perspective, from outside looking in, helped give these waltzes their strangely troubling resonance.

Ravel had still not finished *Daphnis* by 1911, and Reynaldo Hahn, Proust's lover, quickly wrote the Indian fantasy ballet *Le Dieu bleu* for Nijinsky to dance instead. Also to fill the gap left by *Daphnis,* Tchérepnine churned out a short Greek-themed ballet, *Narcisse,* in which Fokine used some of the ideas he had intended for Ravel's score.

1912 was the year of new ballets by Hahn, Debussy, and Ravel. Fokine was furious that Nijinsky's choreography for Debussy's *L'Après-midi d'un faune* took precedence among Diaghilev's projects over his own work with Ravel's *Daphnis.* The latter was to be given at the end of the Paris season, because Fokine was busy with other chores beforehand. This was not only a choreographer's conflict. The conductor of *Daphnis,* Pierre Monteux, was "desolated" as he watched how Diaghilev lost interest in *Daphnis* while he promoted Nijinsky's ballet, especially since he felt that the impresario's lover was a poor choreographer "whose intelligence was mainly in his legs." Monteux recalled that, after first being enthused by Ravel's score, Diaghilev's "fervor for Ravel and his music diminished to such a low pitch that it became most difficult to work as we should have done. All the musicians in the orchestra, and I might say in Paris, knew this was Maurice Ravel's greatest work, and we could not understand this lack of interest on the part of our director. I knew that there was a so-called movement to be rid of Fokine, and to replace him with Nijinsky, but this seemed too far-fetched to me at the time to take seriously."

In addition to Monteux's genius, the orchestra of the Ballets Russes could count on its concertmaster, the noted violinist Gaston Poulet, who was Debussy's choice to premiere his violin sonata and who would go on to a distinguished conducting career. The title roles in *Daphnis* were danced by Nijinsky and Tamara Karsavina, and the scenery and costumes were by Léon Bakst. Fokine found it difficult to rehearse in Paris theaters crowded with Diaghilev's friends, many of whom were "nonstop talkers" like Cocteau and Misia Sert. Photos of dancers from the original production of *Daphnis* show surprisingly hefty women in pseudo-Greek costumes, in an era before the anorexic Balanchine ideal for ballerinas.

Towards the end of the season, wearied by struggles largely of his own creation, Diaghilev suggested canceling the *Daphnis* premiere, but Fokine refused. The dancers found themselves challenged by Ravel's often-changing meters, and the composer would stand backstage during rehearsals, helping ballerinas like Karsavina get the rhythms into their feet. The premiere was slightly postponed, which meant that only two performances of *Daphnis* were given, much to Ravel's regret. Diaghilev seemed to want the ballet to be a failure, scheduling it at the beginning of the evening, before the fashionable part of the audience even arrived in their seats, and planning to start the performance a half-hour earlier than usual, apparently to guarantee audience confusion.

Hearing of his intentions, Fokine shrieked at Diaghilev: "I used words which described his relationship with Nijinsky in plain terms. I shouted that the ballet company was turning from a fine art into a perverted degeneracy." Although Diaghilev was persuaded to program the ballet just before intermission, the company seethed with hatred after Fokine's outburst. Pierre Monteux saw this tirade as the beginning of the end of the Ballets Russes' greatest era.

Although the ballet company was divided between Diaghilev and his lover on one side, and Fokine's supporters on the other, the musical preparation remained excellent, thanks to the conductor's calm mastery. Monteux felt he had enough time to prepare the first and second tableaux of the ballet, but not the third, because "Ravel added voices to the score at a later date." Through all the hysteria, Monteux recalled Ravel as "usually quite undemonstrative." During the most passionate scenes of Slavic fury, the emotional violence seemed only to fascinate him. Ravel admired Nijinsky, and Debussy's score for *L'Après-midi d'un faune,* so that he was unable to feel jealous of Diaghilev's attention to this production; he always said that Debussy's score was the music he would like to hear if he were dying.

Ravel's ballet *Daphnis et Chloé* (1911), from which he drew two orchestral suites, lasts almost an hour. In the action, a group of shepherds are gathered on the island of Lesbos. Daphnis and Dorcon dance in competition for a kiss from Chloé; Daphnis wins and swoons with joy at his reward. But a band of pirates attack the island and carry Chloé off with them. Daphnis is prostrate, but the surrounding statues of nymphs descend from their pedestals and bring Daphnis to a huge rock that changes into the image of the god Pan. Daphnis bows down to him. Meanwhile, the pirates who have kidnapped Chloé compel her to dance and make merry with them. Suddenly Pan appears and the pirates escape, terrified. In the final scene Daphnis and Chloé dance in honor of the love of Pan and Syrinx, and a delirious *danse générale* winds up this ballet firmly based on the panic themes that preoccupied Ravel for his entire career.

The performance was a triumph for connoisseurs like Stravinsky, who called *Daphnis* "one of the loveliest works of French music." But the kudos of the first evening went to Nijinsky in the Debussy ballet, with accolades also reserved for the distinguished dance teacher Enrico Cecchetti, who danced the role of the old shepherd in *Daphnis*. Fokine and his dancers had several curtain calls, but Ravel modestly avoided the ovations. These two performances, which were all that Diaghilev's procrastinations allowed in 1912, were the last time that Nijinsky danced the role of Daphnis. In performances the following season, it was taken over by Fokine.

Daphnis et Chloé is a work to be heard with humility and even a dollop of fear, as its magic force is consequential. Like African deities one doesn't like to stare at in museums, *Daphnis* has deeply magic power. From the introductory hum of expectation, to the use of women's voices like a panic ritual, the score has uncanny verve. Parts of it are as repetitive and insistent as Stravinsky's *Sacre du Printemps*. The work is divided into a dozen sections, with possible numerological significance, harkening back to Ravel's lessons in occult science with Ricardo Viñes.

As ever with Ravel, inspiration from popular music bursts in. The third section of *Daphnis* has burlesque band effects, swelling horns, and chuckling winds to evoke comic drunkenness. In the sixth-movement nocturne, marked "slow and mysterious dance," there is an urgency about the night, a sense of something powerful approaching. The wind becomes a character in the drama, lurching as powerfully as a maritime squall; a high violin shudders, murmurs, and shimmers, like animals out of sight in a forest. Like a magical Greek garden, this nocturne has great mystery, with sighing and groaning women. Ravel would later be intrigued by composers who used cries and groans, like the Italian futurists and his own student, Obouhov, but the vocal effects in *Daphnis* are in fact closer to the Russian orthodox church music of an earlier epoch.

A warrior dance, the eighth movement, shows how Ravel used the orchestra for making war and his chorus for making love. The dance has the orchestral sheen of the Russian composers Ravel loved, and the sweep of Elgar, a composer he admired as "completely Mendelssohn," a term of high praise for him. A swirling "oriental" flute plays whirling dervish melodies, a version of musical possession, with gutteral, visceral cries from the chorus. In the suppliant dance of Chloé, the ninth movement, the violins sigh in unison as the personification of the wilting heroine.

Daybreak, the tenth section of the ballet, is one of its most famous parts. When Ravel later made two orchestral suites from the music of *Daphnis* for concert performance, he began the second suite at this point and ran it on to the end of the ballet. As the sun rises, cyclical figures continue endlessly with the chirping and trilling of birds, and all swells suddenly into a heightened emotionalism as nature renews itself as a caress, a gentle encouragement of the already ardent lyric flow.

The solo flute draws Daphnis's attention to a group of youngsters, among whom Chloé is concealed. The lovers' reuniting is expressed in their own love theme, joined to the music celebrating the dawn; the woodwinds recount the loves of Pan and Syrinx, as lovely and lyrical as can be imagined, followed by the invigorating abandon of the final Bacchanal. Ravel's understanding of ballet was so profound that he was able to transcend the medium. Producing an eminently danceable score, he also wrote what his student Roland-Manuel referred to as a "symphony."

The ballet ends in a general dance with swirling Asian melodies in the Borodin style and forceful playing led by the brass section. Voices come back with a vengeance, sounding like orgasmic shouts. To the public at the premiere, the costumes and scenery of *Daphnis* seemed out of kilter with the music, however lovely most experts found Ravel's achievement. Yet even here there were dissenters: One spectator at the 1913 performances, twenty-two-year-old Soviet composer Sergey Prokofiev, wrote to Tchérepnine that the ballet "left me cold." Thinking that the work was written by Debussy, Prokofiev found it hard "to come to terms with the seeming abundance of water" in the score and found the action at times "impotent and unimaginative." Recorded versions of the suites from *Daphnis* conducted by Cantelli, Monteux, and Toscanini prove the silliness of such criticisms. *Daphnis et Chloe,* likely Ravel's masterpiece, is one of the outstanding musical achievements of the century.

After *Daphnis et Chloé* was completed, Ravel learned from his doctors that he was suffering from "incipient neurasthenia," so he planned a rest cure. In 1913, however, Diaghilev asked him to join Stravinsky in reworking the orchestration of Mussorgsky's *Khovanshchina* for a new production. He found the offer irresistible but refused another Diaghilev request, to orchestrate some Scarlatti sonatas for a ballet, because "I really have better things to do," as he told Stravinsky. Vincenzo Tommasini finally orchestrated the Scarlatti pieces in a ballet, *The Good-Humoured Ladies*. Ravel and Stravinsky worked on *Khovanschchina* in Clarens, Switzerland, during March and April, 1913, although Ravel ended up with the lion's share of the collaboration.

Around this time Ravel sent letters to Igor with a slightly flirtatious tone, like the note from May 1913, with the dateline Hôtel Splendide: "I could leap into your apartment from my balcony, though I would not take advantage of this possibility. From morning on—around 12:30 P.M.—we could exchange flatteries in our pyjamas." And it is true that, on a field trip to buy paper, they shared a bed one night in a cramped hotel that had run out of rooms. However, Stravinsky wrote to the stage designer Alexandre Benois in July 1914, "I love Ravel very much, not sentimentally but actually. . . . He is one of those artists who give me great pleasure." Igor felt it necessary to specify, even ironically, the nature of his love for Maurice. The two men shared some curious interests: Ravel and Stravinsky both had a voyeuristic fascination with things medical, particularly women's surgical experiences. Ravel informed Stravinsky in a 1913 letter that Mrs. Alfredo Casella had been "completely drained and stuffed with absorbent cotton," and that Mrs. Florent Schmitt had an intestinal inflammation following her operation.

While not working on Mussorgsky, Stravinsky showed the as-yet unperformed score of *Le Sacre du printemps* to Ravel, who was enormously excited. Stravinsky later said that Ravel was the only person to realize the importance of *Le Sacre* before it was performed. The savagery and inexorability of the score did not usually inspire immediate affection. Pierre Monteux, who led the premiere, would tell lecture audiences that he "hated" *Le Sacre du printemps* at the time, and that years later he "hated it even more."

Stravinsky also showed Ravel his *Trois poésies de la lyrique japonaise,* describing it as inspired by Arnold Schoenberg's *Pierrot Lunaire,* the score of which he had seen in Berlin. Ravel became fascinated by the new style and soon produced his own *Trois poèmes de Stéphane Mallarmé*. He envisaged a concert that would require a narrator, singer, piano, string quartet, two flutes, and two clarinets, with a program consisting of *Pierrot Lunaire,* Stravinsky's Japanese poems, and his own Mallarmé songs.

The three Mallarmé poems are " Soupir" [Sigh], "Placet futile" [Pointless Petition] and "Surgi de la croupe et du bond" [Sprung up from the Croup and by Leaps and Bounds]. In the first song, Ravel chose a text, like Tristan Klingsor's "Asie," that yearns for nature as a way to escape the constraints of modern civilization, and the writing for strings is particularly close to the Second Vienna school. The second song, *Placet futile,* is a rococo fantasy of eighteenth-century jesting, like the whimsical Verlaine poem "Sur l'herbe," set earlier. Here, however, elegiac music expresses passion through an artificial, affected text. Once again, Ravel was being "sincere in his insincerity. "

The final song, *Surgi de la croupe et du bond,* recounts a bewitched walk in the forest, of a kind found in works by the Second Vienna school from Schoenberg's *Verklärte Nacht* and *Erwartung,* to Alban Berg's *Wozzeck*. The Viennese inspiration for Ravel's songs convinced at least one authority: Anton Webern conducted Ravel's Mallarmé songs in concert because, as the pianist Eduard Steuermann recalled, he "adored them, especially the last, which is very close to Schoenberg."

Curiously, Debussy also made a setting of *Trois poèmes de Stéphane Mallarmé*, at almost exactly the same time, coincidentally choosing two of the same poems as Ravel. Debussy wrote a snitty letter on the subject: "Is it not a phenomenon of auto-suggestion worthy to be transmitted to the Academy of Medicine?" Ravel shrugged off Debussy's irony; as he had written to Cipa Godebski back in 1910, it was important to resist the will of journalists who would be happy to see Fauré, d'Indy, Debussy, and Ravel "give each other jiu-jitsu kicks." (Typically, the energetic little Ravel was up-to-date in his sporting reference; jiu-jitsu had been widely introduced to France as recently as 1905 by Guy de Montgrilhard, a fighter who staged exhibition matches in Paris under the name Régnier, spelled Ré-Nié because he thought it looked more Japanese).

At the same time he was at work on the Mallarmé poems, Ravel composed a brief piano *Prélude* for a women's sight-reading competition at the Conservatoire, a minor piece. He also produced two pastiches in the style of Borodin and Chabrier, inspired by his friend Alfredo Casella's craze for musical pastiche. *A la manière de Borodine* is a light, liltingly descending melody, as in the *Polovtsian Dances,* while *À la manière de Emmanuel Chabrier* is more complex. It is a pastiche of the way Chabrier might have written his own pastiche of an aria from Gounod's *Faust.* This daisy chain of musical parody results in a charming work that captures the shimmering quality of Chabrier's piano writing in works like *Idylle.*

On 29 May 1913, Ravel attended the stormy premiere of *Le Sacre du printemps,* which he was convinced would prove to be "an event as great as *Pelléas.* It was a memorable brawl, and Ravel's friend Valentine Gross, who was present, recalled: "I saw Maurice Delage, beetroot-red with indignation, little Maurice Ravel truculent as a fighting cock, and Léon-Paul Fargue spitting out crushing remarks at the hissing boxes." Florent Schmitt shouted at those who booed, "Shut up, you 16th arrondissement bitches!" People shouted insults, howled and whistled, slapped and punched those they disagreed with. The music was an occasion for panic, for the unleashing of violent emotion. One well-dressed woman called Ravel a "sale Juif."

The violence of *Le Sacre* prefigured the paroxysm of world violence just around the corner, which would sweep up Ravel along with the rest of Europe.

CHAPTER FOUR

Ravel's War

1914–1919

In January 1914, the Mallarmé songs were premiered in Paris, sung by Jane Bathori, and a London premiere quickly followed in March 1915, sung by Bathori and conducted by Thomas Beecham. This was one of the rare occasions when Beecham conducted Ravel's music. As a fervent admirer of Delius, Beecham shared his low view of Ravel.

Two more songs, *Deux mélodies hébraïques,* were completed in 1914. The first, *Kaddisch,* is imposingly liturgical in tone, but with sweetly melodic turns reminiscent of Saint-Saëns's *Samson et Dalila.* There are two "amens" in *Kaddisch,* one in the middle of the text and the other at the end, although in liturgical practice an amen customarily occurs only at the end of a prayer. The florid final amen suggests that Ravel had heard the ornate singing of synagogue cantors, perhaps on recordings. The text here is straightforward, but the second song, *L'Engime éternelle,* is ironical, deflating the faith of the first. The world asks questions, and the only answer it receives is "tra la tra la la la la la," for all the world like Carmen's coquettish "tra la la's" in reply to Don José in Bizet's opera. The first, sober song is in Aramaic, and the second, ironic one is in Yiddish.

Meanwhile, Ravel's international fame continued to grow. The Italian composer Ildebrando Pizzetti wrote in *Musicisti contemporanei* that Ravel's humor was "full of light and brilliant verve, a humorist of the Courteline type rather than the Jules Renard type, almost a caricaturist." Answering those who thought Ravel's music lacked human feeling, Pizzetti argued, "It may not be his fault. And then, who knows? They say he is preparing the music for a *Saint Francis*. Saint Francis! Perhaps Maurice Ravel is preparing to surprise us with burning music of infinite love?" Ravel did speak to friends about the *Fioretti,* but never completed any musical piece inspired by the saint. In 1914 too, Ravel's publisher, Durand, sponsored a full-length study of the composer, the first of many volumes about Ravel, by his pupil and friend Roland-Manuel.

As another guarantor of posterity's interest, a German mechanical piano firm, Welte, invited him, in 1913, to make two recordings as a pianist. The Welte company usually did its recordings in Germany, but they transported the machinery to France for the occasion. (On the same trip they also recorded Debussy, who was thrilled with such technical advances.) In the fall of 1913, Ravel recorded the first two movements of his *Sonatine* and the *Valses nobles et sentimentales.* He would only produce one other brief series of recordings for mechanical piano. He is often wrongly identified as pianist in a series of recorded songs sung by Madeleine Grey, but his interest in the recording medium was lifelong. His second and last series of keyboard recordings in 1922 were for the British affiliate of an American company, Aeolian-Duo-Art. According to cataloguer Jean Touzelet, it is certain that on this occasion Ravel recorded *Oiseaux tristes* and *La Vallée des cloches* from *Miroirs,* and *Pavane pour une infante défunte.* But for the more technically challenging *Toccata,* from *Le Tombeau de Couperin,* and *Le Gibet,* from *Gaspard de la nuit,* he asked the young virtuoso Robert Casadesus to fill in for him, although the records were published as performed by the composer. This sort of imposture would be frequent during Ravel's recording career. For his *Boléro* in 1930, he beat time while an orchestra prepared by another conductor, Albert Wolff, played, but the recording of the Concerto in G, published as conducted by Ravel, was in fact led by the Portuguese conductor Pedro de Freitas-Branco.

Ravel was fascinated by new methods of sound reproduction, served on record prize committees and owned an electrical record player not long after they were invented. He seemed to relish the blind quality of recordings that can mask a true identity. In the early history of recordings, it was not unusual for someone to present himself as someone else entirely, without the public being the wiser. Otherwise, Ravel conducted *Introduction and Allegro* for a recording and the ensemble in *Chansons madécasses,* both in 1932; but he only "supervised" other musicians' work in his Quartet for strings in 1927 and again in 1934, and in *Boléro,* conducted by Piero Coppola in 1930. For this last record, Ravel's participation was mainly in pulling the conductor by the jacket and yelling, "Not so fast!" He also approved recording sessions for *Menuet antique* in 1930, *Pavane pour une infante défunte* in 1932, the *Trois chants hébraïques* also in 1932, and two songs, *Don Quichotte à Dulcinée* and *Ronsard à son âme,* sung by the baritone Martial Singher in 1934 and 1935, respectively. For the listener in search of Ravel performing Ravel, therefore, the pickings are slim, but we may be sure that in his version of *Boléro,* the tempo is as he wished, and he clearly admired a number of musicians he worked with, from Casadeus to Freitas-Branco, and was pleased to endorse them as interpreters.

Soon after the premiere of *Le Sacre du printemps* came the shocking news that Nijinsky had married a woman dancer, and Diaghilev's hysteria was cataclysmic. Diaghilev had planned to travel with Ravel to Lugano, Switzerland, to confer with the designer Alexandre Benois about future projects, but now all plans were postponed. A scheduled ballet by Richard Strauss to a story by Hugo von Hofmannsthal, *La Légende de Joseph,* was salvaged, with Fokine replacing Nijinsky as choreographer. Unlike most of Diaghilev's colleagues, Ravel did not shun the married Nijinsky, who began a rapid mental and physical decline. Diaghilev's associates were barred from working with Nijinsky at the risk of excommunication, but Ravel dared to lend him a helping hand, quickly revising existing orchestrations for Schumann's *Carnaval* and Chopin's *Sylphides* for Nijinsky's ballet troupe in a London performance in March. Getting married had not improved Nijinsky's fragile emotional balance, but Ravel was not repelled by insanity, especially of the Russian variety. He seemed to recognize in Nijinsky, as in Debussy's faun, a fellow denizen of an antique garden where Pan held sway. Unlike Monteux and others, Ravel approved of Nijinsky's choreography, especially in *Daphnis,* and wrote a never-published article saying so, probably at the same time as he made his orchestrations for the dancer.

Ravel in front of his library. Photo inscribed to Louise Alvar. Courtesy of the Charles Alvar Harding collection, on deposit at the Pierpont Morgan Library, New York.

Poster for a Ravel Festival, Hôtel du Palais, August 24, 1930, featuring a bust of Ravel by Louise Ochse. Courtesy of Arbie Orenstein.

Opposite: Program, Concerts-Colonne, Théâtre du Châtelet, pieces by Chabrier, Franck, Dubois, Beethoven, Saint-Saens, and Wagner along with Ravel's *Une Baroque sur l'Océan*, February 3, 1907. Courtesy of Arbie Orenstein.

CONCERTS-COLONNE

(35e ANNÉE)

THEATRE DU CHATELET

Dimanche 3 Février, à 2 h. 1/2

(Seizième Concert de l'Abonnement)

AVEC LE CONCOURS DE M.

JEAN BATALLA

OUVERTURE DE "GWENDOLINE". Emm. CHABRIER.

LES ÉOLIDES................ C. FRANCK.

1re Audition aux Concerts-Colonne.

DEUX PIÈCES EN FORME CANONIQUE. Th. DUBOIS.

1re Audition.

Hautbois : **M. GAUDARD**
Violoncelle : **M. BARETTI**

SYMPHONIE EN UT MINEUR.... BEETHOVEN.

I. *Allegro.*
II. *Andante.*
III. *Scherzo et Finale.*

QUATRIEME CONCERTO Dᵉ PIANO. C. SAINT-SAENS.

M. JEAN BATALLA

UNE BARQUE SUR L'OCÉAN.... Maurice RAVEL.

1re Audition.

LES "MAITRES CHANTEURS". R. WAGNER.

(Ouverture)

LE CONCERT SERA DIRIGÉ PAR M.

GABRIEL PIERNÉ

PIANO ERARD — CELESTA MUSTEL

PRIX DES PLACES

Bureaux et Location : Loges, Baignoires, Balcon, Fauteuils d'orchestre (1re Catégorie), **10 fr.**
Chaises d'orchestre, **8 fr.** — 1re Galerie et Fauteuils d'orchestre (2e catégorie), **6 fr.** —
1er Amphithéâtre et Parterre, 5 fr. — 2e Amphithéâtre, 2 fr. — 3e Amphithéâtre, **1 fr.**
— (Les 2e et 3e Amphithéâtres ne se donnent pas en location.)

Le **Bureau** de Location est ouvert au théâtre du Châtelet, tous les jours de 1 heure à 6 heures
le samedi de midi à 6 heures, et le dimanche de 10 heures à midi.

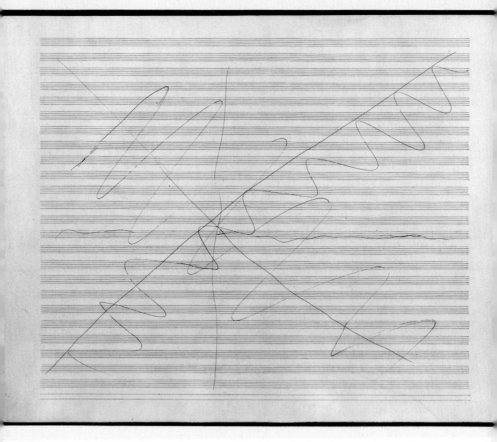

op left: Ravel with Georges Jean-Aubry. Courtesy of the Charles Alvar Harding collection, on
eposit at the Pierpont Morgan Library, New York.

op right: Roland-Manuel and Ravel, 1923, at Lyons-la-Forêt.

ottom: A page (between p. 45 and p. 46) from the autograph manuscript of Ravel's "Concerto pour
1ain gauche seule." Courtesy of the Charles Alvar Harding collection, on deposit at the Pierpont
Morgan Library, New York.

Ravel in overcoat and scarf. Courtesy of the Charles Alvar Harding
collection, on deposit at the Pierpont Morgan Library, New York.

Ravel at Oxford to receive his honorary Doctorate of Music. October 23, 1928.
Courtesy of the Charles Alvar Harding collection, on deposit at the Pierpont
Morgan Library, New York.

avel with Louise Alvar Harding. Courtesy of the Charles Alvar Harding
ollection, on deposit at the Pierpont Morgan Library, New York.

vel postcard photo. Courtesy of the Charles Alvar
rding collection, on deposit at the Pierpont Morgan
brary, New York.

Ravel with Lennox Berkeley. Courtesy
of the Charles Alvar Harding collection, on deposit at the Pierpont Morgan
Library, New York.

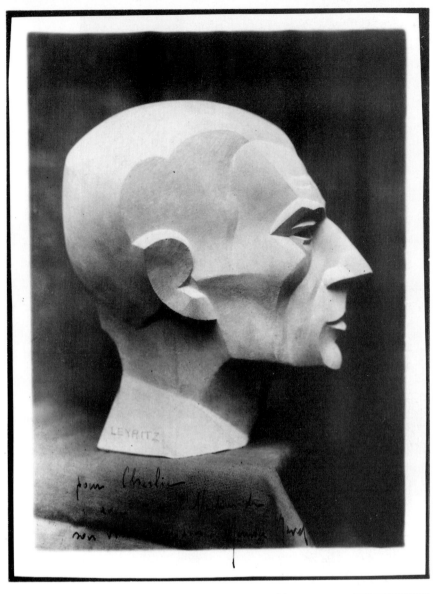

Top: Photo of a bust of Ravel by Leyritz. The handwritten note reads: "To Charlie, with all the affection of his old friend." Courtesy of the Charles Alvar Harding collection, on deposit at the Pierpont Morgan Library, New York.

Ravel holding a wine glass. Courtesy of the Charles Alvar Harding collection, on deposit at the Pierpont Morgan Library, New York.

He wrote to Cipa Godebski in spring 1914, saying that Casella had "photographed us, Nijinsky and me, in the most surprising posture. No doubt he'll show you these singular prints if you ask him." Ravel was referring to a group of photos, including one of himself and Nijinsky playing the piano in his apartment, with a copy of a Greek vase on the piano lid. Another picture showed Ravel with Nijinsky standing on the balcony of the Ravel apartment, always a significant location for the composer. Ravel commented in the same letter on the recent ban of the tango as "lewd" by the Archbishop of Paris. Ravel declared that he was composing another type of dance, a "Forlane," and he would "get busy to have it danced at the Vatican by Mistinguett and Colette Willy in drag." He was clearly amused by the scandal created by Colette when she danced at the Moulin-Rouge in 1907 with her female lover, the cross-dressing Marquise de Belbeuf, who planted a kiss on her lips.

A month after the ballets that Ravel revised for Nijinsky had been performed in London, Diaghilev announced that a Ballets Russes performance of *Daphnis et Chloé* in the same city would omit the choral parts. Ravel copied out for the British press a letter of protest prepared for him in English, perhaps by Georges Jean-Aubry, and asked Vaughan Williams to circulate his message. Diaghilev replied that when the ballet was performed with choruses, the effect was "detrimental." Ravel won his argument and the choruses were used in all major productions of *Daphnis*.

Ravel had reached a level of career success that sparked jealousies. The first volume of Proust's *À la recherche du temps perdu* had just been rejected by the *Nouvelle revue française* at the behest of André Gide. Madame Jean Cruppi, a government minister's wife, wrote to Proust asking for an introduction to the *NRF*, and he replied, in June 1914, "I believe I heard that you had ties with Mr. Ravel, (whose) so remarkable music is very especially appreciated at the *Nouvelle revue française*. And he is praised there with an enthusiasm so rare that it seems difficult to imagine that he does not have ties also with M. Ghéon and M. Rivière. I don't want to say that they praise him out of friendship, they are incapable of it, but except when one lives as I do, in bed, generally one seeks to meet admirers who are so enthused. I think Mr. Ravel would be a perfect introducer."

In fact, Ravel received mixed reviews from the *NRF*, including one by Jacques Rivière that called him inferior to Debussy, and he steered clear of the overtly gay Henri Ghéon, who went cruising for boys with André Gide at steambaths and swimming pools. Proust mixed his jealousy for Ravel with admiration; in 1916 when the writer invited Gaston Poulet's quartet to play in his apartment at 102 boulevard Haussmann, the program included Ravel's *Quartet*.

Ravel is also mentioned in Proust's *Le Temps retrouvé*, at a party where the Duchesse de Guermantes chats with the narrator, Marcel. A young man bothered by their talking moves closer to the musicians, "for they were playing the *Kreutzer Sonata*, but he, having misunderstood the program, thought it was a piece by Ravel that had been described to him as lovely as Palestrina, but hard to understand."

Despite such jokes, at Proust's funeral on November 21, 1922, in the church of Saint-Pierre-de-Chaillot, the *Pavane pour une infante défunte* was played, although it is uncertain whether this odd choice was Proust's own. By an even stranger coincidence, years later Proust's faithful maidservant, Céleste Albaret, eventually became the caretaker of the Ravel Museum at Montfort l'Amaury. Céleste recalled later that Proust had often spoken to her of composers like Debussy, Fauré, "and even Ravel," but she confessed that with museum visitors, she "spoke much more about Mr. Proust than about Ravel."

Although famous enough to inspire Proust's jealousy, Ravel was far from rich. In April 1914 he wrote to his brother, Edouard, who had joined the army, saying that he and their mother didn't have ten francs in the house. In the mid-1920s, when his fame was at a new peak, Ravel earned from his compositions only today's equivalent of about thirteen thousand dollars a year, according to Manuel Rosenthal, who examined his royalty sheets. Touring as a concert performer was one of his few means of earning money, and despite his limitations both as pianist and conductor, Ravel was obliged to tour constantly.

When World War I broke out, Ravel found himself in a creative dilemma. He was working on two long-standing projects of Austrian and German inspiration: Hauptmann's play *The Sunken Bell*, and the orchestral piece *Wien*, a tribute to the Viennese waltz which would emerge years later as *La Valse*. He was also fascinated by the experiments of Schoenberg and the Second Vienna school. Much of his creative path was in the direction of Germany, but suddenly these creators belonged to the enemy side, so Ravel stopped the Hauptmann project and postponed his waltz work.

Instead, in July 1914 he began what would be his last major work for solo piano, *Le Tombeau de Couperin*. In these pieces, which were finished in 1917 and premiered two years later, the composer danced lightly with the ashy taste of death in his mouth. He sketched a funeral urn that was reproduced on the printed version of *Tombeau,* each of whose six sections, *Prélude, Fugue, Forlane, Riagaudon, Menuet,* and *Toccata,* was dedicated to friends killed in the war. As for the title, Ravel said that the piece was not an homage only to Couperin, but to all composers of the eighteenth century.

Still, he knew the music of François Couperin *le Grand,* played for him by the Polish virtuoso Wanda Landowska on her specially built Pleyel harpsichord, which sounded more like a jangly piano than a historically accurate instrument. Landowska recalled that Couperin's *L'Arlequine* was one of Ravel's favorite pieces, and she often played it for him. *L'Arlequine,* the portrait of a female harlequin, is marked to be played "grotesquely," and its strong, mischievous wit has the jaunty grace of a Spanish dance. No doubt Landowska tried, as she did successfully with Manuel de Falla and Poulenc, to commission a new work for her instrument, but Ravel never went further than his song *D'Anne jouant de l'espinette,* which has been recorded using a spinet.

In April 1919 *Le Tombeau de Couperin* was introduced to Paris by pianist Marguerite Long, who soon after decided to omit the final *Toccata* from her concert performances of the piece, as she deemed it too difficult. At the premiere, with Paris under siege from a deadly flu epidemic, Ravel announced to the pianist before the concert, "Something is surely going to happen. Maybe the piano's legs will fall off." So many dead friends were mentioned in the work's dedications that Ravel, ever alert to the supernatural, was ready for poltergeists. The *Tombeau* would gain wider circulation when Ravel orchestrated four of the movements in 1919. There is nothing lugubrious about *Tombeau,* a lilting celebration of life, melody, and Cartesian rigor, which later inspired the choreographer George Balanchine to create one of his greatest ballets. Ravel would be able to joke through the worst of his war experience in letters home, and to observe characteristic details, never losing himself in the chaos. He thereby preserved the life-enhancing, celebratory qualities of his art during the tragic war years.

At almost forty, he made strenuous efforts to join the military, trying for the most dangerous branch of the service, the air force. Ravel had been rejected for military duty years before because of a hernia and general bodily weakness. In letters to friends, he repeated that it wouldn't bother him to die, as he was still in shock after his father's death and worried by his mother's rapidly failing health. He did not wish to survive his parents. Still, he made light of his attempts. In a letter of September 1914 to Roland-Manuel, he wrote with a narcissistic pirouette that the draft board "will finally have to be touched by the grace of my anatomy." He joked to Mrs. Alfredo Casella in a letter from the same month, "I thought I understood that Cocteau was leading herds amid the fields of the Bois de Boulogne, while rereading Virgil." Cocteau was in fact for a brief time assigned the job of cowherd in the Bois de Boulogne; the reference to Virgil was a sly wink at Gide's *Corydon* (1911), named after a character of Virgil's who defended homosexuality. As the war began, Ravel kept his sense of humor enough to chuckle over the mishaps of the artist Aristide Maillol, who got into hot water after Count Harry Kessler cabled him, telling him to bury his statues to preserve them during the coming hostilities, which put the sculptor under suspicion of collusion with the enemy. Ravel wrote to Ida Godebska in September, "No doubt you've heard about the mishaps of poor Maillol, whose innocence almost involved him in an affair of morals, espionage, and art combined. All that, naturally, due to our noble friend Count K[essler]. The details of this story are really funny."

Ravel pulled strings with a friend, the socialist minister and scientist Paul Painlevé, to be admitted to military service, but his desire to be in the air corps was discouraged by all of his important friends. The impulse to offer oneself up for sacrifice was not unusual among artists at the time, and in Ravel's case the compulsion to serve was one of his first public acts of disobedience to his mother's wishes. On August 20, 1914, he wrote to Cipa Godebski, "I know I'm committing a crime." He told Cipa that his wife and children "could, if need be, do without you. Valéry Larbaud leaves a mother who is still young. But me, my mother is a poor old woman who cannot be sustained by either religion or principles, whose sole ideal has always been the love of her husband and children, and who would feel no shame in conserving what remains for her. A sort of monster, right? How many monsters like that exist, and you know how I love this one."

He was obliged to abandon another project, a piano concerto based on Basque themes, entitled *Zaspiak-Bat* [Seven in One], referring to the seven Basque provinces united. And at least one other project, a timely panic subject involving a "Romantic Night, with spleen, infernal hunt, accursed nun, etc.," was never carried further.

He did, however, finish a piano trio, which was first performed in the spring of 1915. One listener on that occasion was the French Catholic writer Charles Du Bos, who remembered how the "entire small group of listeners marvelled at the first movement's opening phrase, not only the jewel of the work, but equal in the domain of pure beauty to any masterpiece of Persian or Japanese art."

The trio is in four movements, *Modéré, Pantoum, Passacaille,* and *Final-Animé*. The work opens with the piano's first chaste statements of refinement and resignation, to which is added the violin's assertiveness. As often in Ravel's music, the violin is the exponent of infectious emotion. The piano's lower range and the cello combine for Slavic dash. The title of the second movement, *Pantoum*, is an Oriental poetic form: Asian-sounding melodies, via Borodin, sinuous melodies and plucked Chinese-sounding effects are plentiful. The passacaglia begins with low piano notes like a somber call to prayer in Russian orthodox ritual, a return to spiritual concentration after the glitz of the pantoum, and with the brief finale we return to the world of shiny, glittering things.

Ravel told the violinist Hélène Jourdan-Morhange that at the beginning of the work, the little notes leading to the violin's singing phrase should be treated "like a Hawaiian guitar's glissando." In the finale, he told her, the pianist must "play the star, and give trumpet accents to his fanfares." Ravel himself thought of his trio as almost too classical, saying ironically, "It's like Saint-Saëns!" At a dinner party years later when Pierre Fournier, Georges Enesco, and Robert Casadesus performed the trio, Gaby Casadesus said that Ravel behaved like a bear in a cage: "He paced up and down, bitterly criticizing the construction of the work being played. He seemed very nervous and just kept repeating that the trio was like Lalo and Saint-Saëns. . . . I was very astonished by this totally inhabitual nervousness, and I wondered if he wasn't ill."

Another Panic work was finished at the beginning of 1915: *Trois Chansons* for unaccompanied voices, with texts written by the composer himself. The folklike songs are *Nicolette, Trois beaux oiseaux de paradis,* and *Ronde.* About the texts, Ravel wrote to Lucien Garban in June 1916: "As for *Trois beaux oiseaux,* it's true that the chorus has no words, but what do you want? We can't exactly have them sing 'shit'—it would be monotonous."

He took special pains over the final *Ronde,* ending with a list of forest enchanters that young maidens should beware of. Ravel enlisted the help of literary friends like Calvo to enumerate the sprites, as if needing to invoke an encyclopedia of these deities before leaving to fight in the forests of France. The bloodbaths of the opening months of the war may have reminded the composer of the violence of Ancient Greek rites. *Ronde* tells us that the woods are full of "satyrs, centaurs, canny warlocks, goblins, incubuses, ogres, imps, fauns, hobgoblins, devils, little devils, devilish imps, goat-feet, gnomes, demons, werewolves, sylphs, surly monks, cyclops, genii, goblins, breton goblins, necromancers, kobolds . . . Ah!"

For Ravel, witchcraft was part of human life, around every corner. He would insist on walking his friend Hélène Jourdan-Morhange to her door late at night, saying, "What if a satyr suddenly burst forth?" In Ravel's imagination, satyrs and goblins did burst forth, although magic in the woods, sometimes somber or tragically violent, is as much a German literary tradition as a French one, and itself derives from Pan worship. The list of magical beings was an extended self-portrait. Indeed, friends like André Suarès often compared Ravel to one or another of these goblins: "Standing up," wrote Suarès, "he seemed almost a dwarf, a big-headed kobold."

Rejected by the air force at the behest of influential friends, who were shocked at the idea of his throwing himself into danger, Ravel was given the official excuse that he had been diagnosed with " a hypertrophy of the heart" which he hadn't had six months before. So he became a driver transporting war material and dubbed his car Adelaïde in honor of the "language of flowers." He described to a friend the effect of driving through a war-torn area, "horribly deserted and mute. . . . I don't think I'll ever feel a deeper and stranger emotion than this kind of mute terror."

Settling into his duties, Ravel was stationed at some distance from the front and assigned company in the form of a German captive, as he informed his friend Lucien Garban: "Now there's two of us to yawn, to have the shit bored out of us, to read detective novels. . . . Our lieutenant is more and more loveable: He reawakens our ardor for chores by calling us "cunts" and "receptacles for balls."

Among his regular correspondents was the mother of Roland-Manuel, Madame Dreyfus, who sent him things to eat and wear. In March 1916 he described leaving on a night mission dressed "as if for a carnival dance, helmeted for a stroll on the rue de la Paix." He wrote asking for a "clothes caprice: leggings," as local stores only sold "odious rigid spats such as I left at home, which make you feel like you have two wooden legs," and thanked her profusely for food packages, with one exception: "One thing, I don't like eel. . . . To tell the truth, I've never been able to eat them, any more than snails or frogs." Another letter was interrupted when he heard some "little cries. . . . It's a poor mouse who's been caught in a rat trap."

Maurice Delage tried, to no avail, to lure Ravel to serve in his division, where soldiers were allowed the use of a piano. In March 1916, Ravel received a letter from his mother, whose health was failing, written in an endearingly illiterate French. Hovering behind the scenes like the mother of Bizet's Don José, she was worried about Maurice's health: "Je ne dors pas j'ai des cochemas" [I'm not sleeping, I have nightmares—with "cochemas" a misspelling of *cauchemars;* she didn't know how to spell words like *shirt* or *pyjama* in French]. The intelligent, capable, and generous Madame Dreyfus became a surrogate mother as Ravel's own mother failed. He became more philo-Semitic, touched by the kindness of his adopted Jewish family, and he developed into an amateur of the history and lore of East European Jewry, charming Jewish friends by telling them about customs in the Jewish community of Lemburg (Lvov), or the theory that in ancient China, Jews were considered an aristocratic class.

Deprived of music, Ravel retained his identity by immersing himself in nature. He slept wrapped in animal skins and was photographed in a bushy fur overcoat, looking like a forest animal. He called these photos "me as a beastie." He noted birdsongs, and retained an obsession with childhood and toys, writing to Madame Dreyfus in August 1916, "I installed two orderlies, a foot soldier and a dragoon, on the door of my gas storage tank.

These orderlies are admirably disciplined, and passively obedient. They are made of pasteboard. On the way back to my room, I saw that alpine soldiers were stationed in the barn, busy playing with little soldiers, also made out of cardboard. . . . If the war lasts any longer, it will be necessary to distribute baby dolls and rattles to the Army of the Republic."

Correspondence was a safety valve. In June 1916, he wrote to Ida Godebska, saying that the soldiers had complained about insufficient food, and the brigadier's reply was, "I don't give a fuck. Let them eat shit!" Ravel noted, "A great eighteenth-century lady said the same thing, although not in those exact words, and maybe that's all we gained by the Revolution." He recounted to Ida a grisly battlefield anecdote, which he described as a "charming after-dinner story" that he would save for postwar social events: "Sent to look for the cadavers of a major and some stretcher bearers," a fellow soldier was "ready to return, his car full of stiffs, when someone pushed at him a fairly large beefsteak wrapped in a piece of cloth, saying, "Take that too, it's the Major."

In 1916 the National League for the Defense of French Music advocated banning all music by recent German and Austrian composers, after the enemy forces deliberately aimed missiles at French cathedrals. The petition, sponsored by Saint-Saëns among others, would not have applied to Bach or Schubert, only modern musicians. Ravel refused to sign, pointing out that not only Schoenberg and Richard Strauss, but Béla Bartók and Zoltan Kodály as Hungarians, would be shunned98 as enemies. He wrote to Roland-Manuel in June 1916 about the French patriots in the National League for the Defense of French Music: "My goodness, I think it would be fine if we were allowed to keep our guns after the war. There will still be things for us to do here. My own role will be simple: I'll barrel in there with my truck." He was ready to run over the offensive Germanophobes.

Ravel's concern about his mother's decline was complicated by his own health problems. He had a bout of dysentery, followed, in September 1916, by an operation in which part of his lower bowel was removed. Ravel wrote to his friend Lucien Garban on September 24, "Don't worry, they haven't taken out all my bowels, only a little bit. I wasn't that heavy beforehand." Garban must have jokingly asked if the nurse was pretty, because Ravel noted, "As for the nurse, she's a lovely damozel, at least a meter taller than I am, charming, full of solicitude, only she has an ugly mug and is over fifty-five years old."

While convalescing in a ward where smoking was allowed, Ravel devoured books like Alain-Fournier's *Le Grand Meaulnes*, a story of boyhood which he hoped one day to adapt as a work for piano or cello and orchestra. He wrote letters to Madame Dreyfus with painful puns: "The face of our brave concierge is often rather highly colored, and sometimes he even crosses the Rubicund." He added a biblical reference, "I savored some lentils yesterday evening. They made me understand Esau, who until now I had always thought a nitwit. Tonight, an egg. Tomorrow, a little veal. I'm heading step by step toward crayfish."

He also had dark moods, writing to Hélène Casella in October 1916 that his fellow soldiers were "rebellious, obscene, stupid, blindly pessimistic, low egoists." And in December he wrote sombrely to his captain: "I really feel that I will never recover. I tried to work a little—impossible. I'm bored wherever I go. At home there's the sad spectacle of my poor mother, weaker and weaker."

His mother's death on January 5, 1917, at the age of seventy-six, was devastating, and Ravel wrote little for three years thereafter, though not from lack of trying. Less than two weeks after his mother's demise, on January 17, he accepted a new proposal from Diaghilev to compose a Futurist ballet in collaboration with the Italian writer Francesco Cangiullo, a friend of Marinetti's. Cangiullo later recalled that the ballet was to be called *The Zoo*, featuring "fantastic fauna" designed by the Italian artist Depero, but Ravel's persistent weakness, even after he had left the army, prevented it from being written. Yet the sad event also proved a form of liberation in his private life. Until his mother's death, believed friends like David Diamond, Ravel had had no sexual release but enjoyed playing games and teasing in compensatory ways.

One such typical tease was in a letter to Roland-Manuel from March 1917, in which he asked about the premiere of his student's first symphonic work, *The Viceroy's Harem,* played in a piano arrangement for four hands, by the composer and Ricardo Viñes. Ravel took the occasion to crack a few phallic jokes: "My dear Brigadier, I'm glad you're satisfied with the guardian of your harem. I'll try, if I may say so, to remain hard-on the job at my new post." He called it a "sensational attraction" that a harem should be presented by Roland-Manuel "and a neuter," meaning Viñes. Ravel jokingly cast himself as a eunuch, the guardian of Roland-Manuel's harem, who was striving to maintain an erection, while the "neuter" Viñes performed the work.

In June 1917, during a temporary leave, Ravel rested at the home of Madame Dreyfus, where he finished *Le Tombeau de Couperin,* begun in 1914. After his mother's death, he could no longer bear to live in the family apartment on the avenue Carnot, so he and Edouard moved to Saint-Cloud, where they lived with surrogate parents, Mr. and Mme. Bonnet.

Trying to survive the effects of his war service, Ravel was assailed by Cocteau, whose own wartime activities included being an inspector of showers for the troops, a duty he performed so assiduously and seductively that he ran into problems with army commanders. Cocteau wrote to the painter Jacques-Emile Blanche in November 1917, calling Ravel "a trained dog . . . that dry farter who splits Mélisande's hairs into a thousand strands and throws his powder in our eyes; still, he's a pretty one, sort of like Bonnard, but less sensitive." Cocteau's was not the only dissenting voice. In the same year Frederick Delius complained in a letter to the British composer Peter Warlock that instead of containing poetry and emotion, Ravel's music, like that of Debussy, was "killed" by the "dross of technic...or they seize upon one little original streak and it forthwith develops into an intolerable mannerism."

In 1918 all that the still-fatigued Ravel achieved was an orchestral transcription of *Alborada del gracioso.* He also wrote his strangest, most discordant work, a brief *Frontispice,* for a book by the Italian poet Ricciotto Canudo (1877–1923), who outspokenly defended bisexuality in his notorious *Futurist Manifesto of Lust.* A survivor of trench warfare in the war, Canudo published a book, *S.P. 503: Le Poème du Vardar suivi de la Sonate à Salonique.* A portrait of Canudo by Picasso decorated the book, whose title page shows a muscled nude youth, wearing a World War I doughboy's hat, blowing a hunting trumpet, straddling a galloping horse, which drools. The jarring sense of a world gone awry is audible in *Frontispice,* which sounds like two pianists playing entirely unconnected pieces until, oddly, a fifth hand enters the aural scene, playing by itself. This five-handed piece is spookily unreal, as if flouting nature and the number of hands that normally occur on human arms.

Early in 1919 Ravel took a much-needed mountain cure at Mégève in the Haute-Savoie region. He wrote to Lucien Garban in February, "Every fifteen minutes you hear the noise of an avalanche: it's the snow piled up on the roofs which suddenly gives way, without warning. It makes a change from Big Bertha." By now a confirmed philo-Semite, his jokes in letters to friends about Jewish-related projects had a relaxed, self-mocking air. He asked Garban to send him the first eight measures of his second Hebraic song, *L'Enigme éternelle,* joking, "with the text in Yiddish, or 'boche' [German], I forget which." When he received the song from Garban in March, he joked again, "You'll see, they're going to commission me to write the Zionist hymn."

Without his parents to deceive any more about his personal life, he was clearly at an emotional turning point. Against his best expectations, he had survived the war and needed to make choices about the life he planned to lead. Marrying a woman was out of the question. When Hélène Casella announced that her marriage to composer Alfredo Casella was over, Ravel wrote back in January 1919 with sympathy, saying, "We artists are not made to marry. We are rarely normal and our lives are even less so." Situating himself in an "abnormal" majority, he found comfort with friends, pets, and his garden. When he returned to Saint-Cloud, he was visited by the journalist Mischa Lévy, to whom he displayed his garden, filled with "large white fantastic flowers." The reporter noted that Ravel patted a dog whose mother was a wolf: "'Yes, yes—a real she-wolf; ha-ha!'—and his small eyes shine with that fanaticism which is typical of him."

He did not spend time in recriminations against the former enemy. Although not a Wagnerian, Ravel went to applaud in June 1919 when, for the first time since the war, Wagner was played in the Tuileries Gardens. He clapped loudly to oppose French patriots who still wanted to ban German music.

At the end of 1919, in the home of a friend in the Ardèche region, he orchestrated the accompaniments to the songs, *Kaddisch* and *L'Enigme éternelle*. He also sketched a new work commissioned by Diaghilev, *La Valse,* which he had been thinking of (and indeed working on in the form of *Wien*) since 1906. Although slowly returning to work, he still mournfully considered that his late mother's "infinite tenderness" had been, in retrospect, his "only reason for living."

CHAPTER FIVE

Le Boeuf sur le Toit

1920–1925

In January 1920 Ravel was awarded the Legion of Honor, which he refused, causing some scandal. In a letter to Roland-Manuel, he compared Legion of Honor recipients to "morphine addicts, who do everything, even trickery, to make others share their passion, perhaps to legitimize it in their own eyes." He added that it would be simple to retract the award as a printing error with the correction, "Instead of Maurice Ravel, read Maurice Rostand." Rostand was one of the most flamboyantly visible gay men of early-twentieth-century Paris, the son of the late Edmond Rostand, author of *Cyrano de Bergerac*. With his hair permed and dyed blond so as to better resemble his idol, Sarah Bernhardt, he lisped, minced, and limped his way through Paris society, resembling "a fat woman dressed as a bellhop in a revue," according to one observer. Rostand's search for sex in public urinals, including one right outside his apartment window, shocked even Cocteau, who decided that Maurice represented "what he did not want to become." By substituting this notorious queen for himself, Ravel was comparing the libido for glory in Legion of Honor recipients to rapacious and visible sexual habits. He saw the Legion of Honor as a silly kind of drag, suitable for a flamboyant type like Rostand, but not for a discreet, disciplined fellow like himself.

Award or not, Ravel's fame was by now considerable. The British theatrical producer Basil Dean was looking for a composer of stage music for James Elroy Flecker's play *Hassan,* and Flecker's widow, Helle, wrote to Dean saying that Ravel's name had been suggested to her in Paris salons. "A composer with a name like his will look well on the programme, whether his music be suitable or not, which few people can tell," she stated. Ravel was told that Flecker was "one of England's most appreciated poets," and he asked to see a French translation of *Hassan.*

Flecker's play, vaguely derived from the *1001 Nights,* offered luxurious, pseudo-Oriental decadence, but the writer's life and work were studded with a kind of overt, grim eroticism that probably would have embarrassed Ravel. Flecker had flamboyant gay affairs at Oxford circa 1900, and *Hassan* features plenty of flagellation, with prisoners tortured to death by a cruel Caliph, since Flecker believed that there is "no great book without its whipping." Perhaps fortunately, Basil Dean decided Delius's music would suit the play better.

Although the Great War was over, death was still present on Ravel's horizon. In September 1920 he lost Pierre Haour, a friend from the *Apache* days. Ravel wrote to Lucien Garban in September 1920 about the failing Haour: "What's devastating is that he won't even have that feeling of well-being in his last moments."

After Haour's death, Ravel took refuge in small pleasures of life, like cigarettes and coffee. He wrote to Garban to say he'd come for a visit "if you have a tobacconist's at the end of your street" and asked for some good coffee, or else his maid, Marie-Thérèse, would in mock-suicide "pass a handsaw, which is all we have here as a sword, through her body."

The comforts of domesticity included a house. When Ravel's artist uncle Edouard died in 1920, he left a modest legacy, enough to buy a small home outside Paris, and Ravel chose a suburb at Montfort-l'Amaury, difficult to reach by train and cab although only thirty miles west of the city. Offering fine balcony views and a pleasant garden, essential requirements for Ravel, the house also had tiny rooms which were cold, dark, and damp. It required renovation to make it habitable, such as putting an indoor staircase between the first and second floors. The sheltered existence he would lead there was necessary after the shocks of the war, which had compromised his health, and the deaths of his parents.

Ravel dubbed his home Le Belvédère, and furnished it with bibelots and curios in a taste that he laughingly called that of "a provincial old maid." There were fake Chinese works of art, ersatz Greek designs, and a number of cheap dolls and automata. Ravel enjoyed spoofing visitors' pretensions by showing off a glass globe and, after hearing coos of admiration, exclaiming "But it's a burned-out light fixture!" Presenting crudely painted canvases as originals by Renoir or the fashionable Italian Monticelli, Ravel would wait for his visitors to murmur polite admiration, then crow, "They're all fakes!" After strenuous objections by the art-loving Hélène Jourdan-Morhange, he agreed to remove the egregious fake Renoirs, "but only to please you," he insisted.

A true image remained above his piano, a pastel portrait of his mother, done by his Uncle Edouard in 1885, when she was forty-five. The swarthy Basque woman looks like a puffy veteran singer in the role of Carmen. There was also the Neptune-like portrait of Joseph Ravel, painted by Desboutin in 1896, and paintings by Tanzy of Maurice at the age of eleven and his brother, Edouard.

Visitors to Le Belvédère have compared it to the home of Des Esseintes in Huysmans's *A rebours,* yet Ravel's house lacks the sense of sadistic danger and abuse of nature typified by Des Esseintes's jewels embedded in a live tortoise's shell. Ravel's taste was twee and kitsch, running more to playful little miniature objects that relaxed and delighted him. Like a child, he adored his toys and bibelots, including a mechanical bird he named Zizi, French slang for penis. When the bird moved and sang on command, Ravel would cry with pleasure, "I can hear his heart beating!" Among his toys were a small boat in which little Japanese figures rowed as they put out their tongues, as well as a box from which a creature's arms, legs, and tongue emerged to waggle with epileptic abandon when a handle was turned. Further comfort and amusement were provided by a trio of much-loved cats, of whom the undisputed star was Mouni. The new homeowner was photographed patting his pet affectionately.

He carefully painted Doric column designs on the walls and decorated a chair back with an ancient Greek-style design of a muse dressed in veils playing the Pan pipes, similar to the Pan figure on the cover of the printed score of the *Menuet antique.* He had an elaborate garden planted, including Japanese bonsai trees, which he admired for their "concentrated power." His decoration of the house has parallels with Alexander Pope's eighteenth-century grotto at Twickenham, where the poet designed a specially lit rock formation embedded with glittering stones, amid ingenious waterworks with dripping murmurs that would have appealed to the composer of *Jeux d'eau*. Pope's shell temple, obelisk in memory of his mother, and other decorations at Twickenham are forerunners of Ravel's gently eccentric house and garden at Montfort. The tradition of a dandy's home, created by exquisite British bachelors like Pope, Horace Walpole, and William Beckford, was imitated by Ravel, who was of course fascinated by English dandies, starting with Beau Brummel.

In his music library, Ravel's collection of scores included only a few sonatas and symphonies of Mozart, which was odd considering his love for that composer, but he owned the scores of several Rameau operas and many works by Bach. Although he had only a few albums of piano pieces by Schubert, Schumann, and Chopin, there was lots of Liszt, in different editions. Wagner was nowhere to be found, although he did have a copy of Meyerbeer's *Le Prophète,* which he said was "infinitely better orchestrated than *Lohengrin,*" and Mendelssohn's piano music in an edition which he prepared himself in 1921. His collection of French music concentrated on Chabrier and Saint-Saëns, as well as colleagues and pupils; he owned scores of songs by Berg and Schoenberg, and the *Kammersinfonie* (1916) by Franz Schreker which sounded Ravelian to some listeners.

Among the books in his library were old memoirs which he loved, like those by Madame de Genlis and the Comtesse de Boigne. When a friend and neighbor, the writer Jacques de Lacretelle, praised the early-nineteenth-century writer Madame de Staël,

Ravel replied that he preferred Madame de Staal de Launay, whose eighteenth-century memoirs, a portrait of court life at the "miniature Versailles" of Sceaux, were praised by Sainte-Beuve as "a fairy tale with a human ending." (Lacretelle, a close friend of the composer, was also a very discreet homosexual.) The library also contained the works of Proust and a Bible, although Manuel Rosenthal, knowing his antichurch attitudes, could not imagine where he got it. Ravel also liked to read erotica, stories and poems in little editions of eighteenth-century smut, with spicy period illustrations, in which sex was distanced, miniaturized, and put under control.

His large record collection included hundreds of 78 RPM discs of classical music, popular songs, and the spoken word. He had records of music by Fauré, Debussy, and Caplet, and younger composers like Poulenc and Milhaud. There was nothing by Beethoven, Bach, Schubert, or Schumann. He did have Moritz Moszkowski's *Danses espagnoles,* Ernesto Lecuona's *Jungle Drums* conducted by Guy Lombardo, excerpts from Shostakovich's *Age of Gold,* Alexandre Mossolov's *Steel Foundry,* and organ recordings by Charles Tournemire. Among records of vocal music, he had the best French classical song composers, as well as lighter items like Reynaldo Hahn's operetta *Brummel,* in honor of Ravel's hero Beau Brummel. There were works by less familiar songwriters, like Louis Beydts's *Le Moineau,* Alfred Bruneau's *L'Attaque du moulin,* (a setting from *Don Quixote*), Szulc's *Divin Mensonge,* Heinrich Proch's *Thème et variations,* and Xavier Leroux's *Le Nil,* sung by Ninon Vallin.

Among recordings of theater, Ravel owned Cocteau's monologue *La Voix humaine,* acted by Berthe Bovy, Molière's *L'Ecole des femmes,* Marcel Pagnol's *Topaze,* Beaumarchais's *Le Barbier de Séville,* and speeches from Racine's *Andromaque* and *Bérénice.* In the spoken-word category he also had *The Trial of Louis XVI,* and Saint Thérèse of Lisieux's writings read by the actress Madeleine Renaud. He owned records of folk music from Egypt, Normandy, Romania, and Kurdistan. In a large collection of variety and popular songs, Ravel favored the records of the singer-songwriter Jean Tranchant, an upper-class crooner. There were also records of the Kentucky Singers doing *The Tiger Rag* and *Tyrolian Song,* as well as vaudeville monologues like G. Chepfer's *Cousin de Molsheim,* with a comic Alsatian accent. Other favored variety performers include the Wal-Berg trio, Noël-Noël, and Paul Colline, a singer of Montmartre songs.

When mealtime rolled around at Le Belvédère, Ravel was a voracious meat eater. Once, offered a vegetarian dinner at a rich lady's house during a concert tour, he left complaining, "Everyone knows I'm a carnivore!" and had his driver phone ahead to his hotel to have a steak ready on his arrival. At home he often gorged on meat. Jourdan-Morhange stated, "Nothing was sadder than to find Ravel alone, seated with his face to the wall, I mean right against the wall, with his back to the window and voraciously eating a much too thick, nearly raw beefsteak." He became house-proud, joking in a letter of July 1924 to Ida Godebska, whose house in the Var region was grandly named Villa Ker-Mireille, "If I rename Le Belvédère, I'll call it Schloss Medina-Cali or else Grandpa's Mosque."

The house at Montfort-l'Amaury was the base for giddy outings to nearby sites of "touristic interest" with Jourdan-Morhange, such as the former home of the mass murderer Landru, who later

109

inspired Chaplin's film *Monsieur Verdoux*. If there was no time to drive to Landru's house, the friends would make a mock pilgrimage to the closer house of Marcelle Tinayre, a popular author of sentimental kitsch. Parisian relaxations included the Empire Music Hall, where Ravel applauded Barbette, a male acrobat born Vander Barbette who performed in blond-wigged drag and who was a favorite of Cocteau's, and Little Tich, "an eccentric dwarf whose performance mixed comedy with pathos." Little Tich may have inspired a project from around 1920 for a fifteen- or twenty-minute ballet for the dancer Sonia Pavlov. *Le Portrait de L'Infante* is said to have been for two dancers, a princess and an acrobatic dwarf. According to the biographer José Bruyr, the work was finished except for the "orchestration" but was never performed or published and is now in a private collection. Its very existence suggests a personal identification with the stunted Little Tich.

Frenetic work and pleasures took their toll. In April 1920 Ravel wrote to Lucien Garban that he promised to change his lifestyle: "It's not that I'm afraid of croaking, on the contrary, but it's starting to be unbearable: the clearest symptoms of neurasthenia, insomnia, nightmares, extreme lassitude on awakening—when I manage to sleep. The desire to do myself in, etc., etc."

His fatigue obliged him to defend himself against intrusive students, particularly women admirers, like the American pianist and conductor Ethel Leginska. He wrote to Hélène Casella, asking her to come to his house to "help me to send away quicker an American woman. To get rid of her, I promised to examine a symphonic poem she wrote. This young person came to live in Montfort in hopes that I'd work with her. You can imagine how I set her straight!" In October 1921 Ravel wrote to Florent Schmitt, passing the buck: "I've persuaded Miss Ethel Leginska that your teaching is much better than mine. Have you seen this young Yankee?"

Gossip was still a passion. He wrote breathlessly to Roland-Manuel in August 1921: "More news since yesterday. [My Czech servant] Prohaska has dumped me suddenly. She wasn't gone for five minutes before I heard that she was the sole client of all the bistros in Montfort, which explains the intermittent nervousness from which many pieces of crockery suffered, and the sudden changes of mood that I attributed to her Slavic origins. All I need is to discover a fetus in the salt box and the complete works of Valentine de Saint-Point missing." Saint-Point was an advocate of Futurist and symbolist dance who gave public lectures, while holding a tiny marmoset by a chain, on subjects like: "At what age should we teach lewdness to our daughters?"

From his aerie at Montfort-l'Amaury, Ravel kept an amused eye on Paris musical scandals. In 1921 he attended a notorious Futurist concert by Luigi Russolo featuring noise machines, cooers, snorers, gulpers, and other effects. A year later he chuckled when Erik Satie was dragged into court by a critic, Jean Poueigh, to whom he had written, "Sir, you are nothing but an asshole, and an unmusical one at that." Satie was sentenced to eight days in prison for defamation, although he was never incarcerated. Ravel's reaction was to send Roland-Manuel a newspaper clipping that quoted Satie on another occasion: "Physically the critic looks serious, as he's a type of contrabassoon." Ravel cut off part of the word *contrabassoon,* making the critic into "a type of cunt" [con], and wondered innocently if there would now be a new Satie trial.

He also made trips to Paris for other cultural events, like the cinema. In February 1922 he saw *The Cabinet of Doctor Caligari,* at a swanky private screening, and he wrote to his friend Georgette Marnold about the luxurious conditions of the show: "I'm a sort of King Ludwig II of Bavaria type, only less loony, at least until now. And for the first time, I've seen real cinema." The comparison to Ludwig, the patron of Wagner and builder of groteque fantasy castles, was probably more a reference to decadent luxury than to the king's homosexuality.

Nevertheless, Ravel's reticence about his emotional life continued to fascinate his friends. In May 1922, after a visit to Montfort, Cocteau wrote to Gide, then embroiled in the controversy over his reprinted gay tract, *Corydon,* telling him that he was Ravel's "favorite bedside author. . . . You are there next to *Adolphe,* which only proves that I am proving nothing." Alongside *Corydon* and Benjamin Constant's eighteenth-century novel lay a copy of *Si le grain ne meurt,* in which Gide openly discussed his passion for Arab boys. Ravel owned one of the first, privately printed copies of *Si le grain ne meurt,* as David Diamond recalled, as well as Edouard Bourdet's *La Prisonnière,* a scorching lesbian drama. Diamond says that the conductor Dimitri Mitropoulos, who was himself gay and convinced that Ravel was too, reported discussions in which Ravel, though always a little afraid of Gide, was impressed by his honesty in admitting his sexual relations with boys. Diamond adds, "The men and women who were bisexual or homosexual, who knew Ravel, never doubted that he was gay, but the straights denied everything." Some heterosexual friends like Alexandre Tansman, however, told Diamond that Ravel was "very discreetly interested in young men."

In the early twenties, Ravel made many trips to London, where he stayed at the home of Louise Alvar, a Swedish soprano who had married an Englishman named Harding. Mrs. Harding would host dinners at which people like Ravel's friend Georges Jean-Aubry, the French biographer and translator of Joseph Conrad, would be present. Conrad himself and Paul Valéry were frequent houseguests.

Ravel also enjoyed playing with his hostess's children. Charles Alvar-Harding, Louise's son, said that Ravel's behavior recalled Puck in *A Midsummer Night's Dream.* Despite his white hair, Ravel was always playing "like another child. . . . With a napkin and an orange he used to perform an explosive trick called the sea-sick Chinaman and I made him waste many oranges by repeating it." Once Charles replaced the seat of Ravel's dining-room chair with flimsy green material, then hid behind a curtain to watch the results of his prank: "Ravel, after recovering from his fall, seemed as amused as I was, and interceded successfully on my behalf" with the boy's appalled parents. Alvar-Harding added that Ravel "spent a good part of his time with me playing another destructive game called water war. Protected by mackintoshes, we hurled at each other sponges heavy with water. Ravel is a terribly bad shot, so the patience of my parents was sorely tried when they saw huge splotches of water on the walls." The players excused themselves by explaining that they were "merely enacting *Jeux d'eau.*"

Ravel relished this sort of violent horseplay while composing *L'Enfant et les sortilèges,* but with adults he acted the role of narcissist, writing to Louise Alvar in September 1922 that photos of him she had sent might be haggard projections of what he could

113

look like twenty years later: "I've received, alas, the photos from London. These Ravels of 1944 are rather troubling, but the others from Holland Park, because not posed for, are less cruel." He shared his moods freely with Louise, writing in July 1925: "My crisis of perversion has not yet been calmed." A neat little cigarette burn on the letter shows that Ravel was smoking, as usual, when he penned it.

London was also a place for musical research. In 1921 Ravel was invited by the conductor and composer Eugène Goossens to meet musicians in the studio of a rich amateur composer and eccentric, George Davison, who had purchased an Aeolian pipe organ. Ravel was especially fascinated by its celesta, chimes, harp, and "echo-organ" effects. The conductor Adrian Boult arrived, pushing his bicycle through the front door, but Ravel stayed at the organ, and only when Malipiero and Manuel de Falla, the latter in London for the British premiere of his *Nights in the Gardens of Spain,* entered did Ravel abandon the instrument. Ravel never wrote anything for the organ but later enjoyed imitating its effects in orchestral works, not least in *Boléro.*

Ravel finished orchestrating *La Valse* by spring of 1920, and he played it to Diaghilev in a two-piano version with Marcelle Meyer. Misia Sert, Stravinsky, and Francis Poulenc were also present. Diaghilev, presumably still steamed about Ravel's work with Nijinsky, rejected *La Valse,* calling it "a masterpiece, but it's not a ballet. It's a portrait of a ballet." Stravinsky did not utter a word in Ravel's defense, and Misia, although she later claimed to have fought Diaghilev "tooth and nail" unsuccessfully on Ravel's behalf, said nothing either. She enjoyed saying that in his music Ravel "puts in the punctuation, but forgets to write the words," an insult that Cocteau noted in his journal decades later. She once described *Daphnis et Chloé* as "rather uneven, but [it] contains ten minutes of music so ideal that they alone would suffice for a composer's immortality."

In his own accounts of this episode, Poulenc, who hankered after a ballet commission from Diaghilev, was titillated and thrilled by Diaghilev's opinion and took a certain joy in Ravel's misfortune. Years later he admitted that Balanchine's choreography for a ballet version of *La Valse* (1951) was one of the strongest dance events he had witnessed, accepting that the piece was a ballet after all. At the time Poulenc was impressed with Ravel's "calm" reaction. The composer simply took his score and walked out, but this understated, repressed response was likely a sign of cold fury.

La Valse begins with faraway spooky murmurs, rustles of ball gowns, like the ghosts of waltzes past. These strangely disconcerting sounds are played by double basses, with mutes on. Bits of swirling melodies are overheard, as in Liszt's *Valse oubliée,* but Ravel's work is far more dynamic, a source of terror. Whizzing by on a whirlwind, these waltzes are as uncontrollable as nightmares. Their magic effect is enhanced by drunken-sounding harmonies, as if a well-watered night on the town had gone wrong. All of the instruments sound ill at ease or out of sorts: the harps are aggressive, the oboes piercing. The piece is divided into two great sections, each of which attains a mighty climax. The mastery of instrumental writing adds to the impression of inexorability.

Ravel subtitled his work, "Choreographic Poem for Orchestra" and added to the score an evocative program of sorts:

"Through clouds whirling around, flashes of light permit us to see waltzing couples. They thin out, by and by, and we can see an immense hall crowded with a rotating throng. The stage gets progressively brighter. Light from chandeliers bursts from the ceiling. An imperial court around 1855."

The violence and operatic distortion of this description suggests that a great dance form has somehow gone astray, conforming to other ills of western civilization. Indeed, in explaining his work, Ravel went outside western tradition to compare his waltzing dancers to dervishes. Between the time he wrote *Adélaïde, ou le langage des fleurs,* which is filled with nostalgia for his grandparents' era of courtship, and the time when he wrote *La Valse,* some nightmarish things had clearly happened. Critics tend to assume that *La Valse* is a product of the war, yet perhaps the emotional disaster of losing his parents was even more decisive. After all, another work explicitly dedicated to men lost in the war, *Le Tombeau de Couperin,* has nothing of the horrific quality of *La Valse.* The composer's student Roland-Manuel referred to the choreographic poem as a *danse macabre,* and we may hear in it a shudder of death's horror.

Ravel returned to Paris to attend the orchestral premiere of *Deux mélodies hébraïques,* sung by Madeleine Grey and conducted by Rhené-Baton. In 1920 he traveled to Vienna, where he was disappointed not to meet Arnold Schoenberg, who was then in Amsterdam as resident composer with Willem Mengelberg's Concertgebouw Orchestra. Ravel stayed for three weeks in the apartment of Alma Mahler, the widow of the composer Gustav Mahler, who was tiring of her relationship with the architect

Walter Gropius and starting to heat up her new sexual conquest, the novelist Franz Werfel.

Alma had a chance to study Ravel at close quarters. He came to breakfast each morning wearing rouge on his cheeks, perfumed and wrapped in an elegant dressing gown, and she concluded, "He was a narcissist. . . . He loved the bright satin robes that he wore in the morning. He related all things to his bodily and facial charms. Though short, he was so well proportioned, with such elegance and such elastic mobility of figure, that he seemed quite beautiful." She noted his taste for "sophisticated kitsch," a "perverted mask" then worn by Paris's avant-garde young musicians. Whatever her other faults may have been, Alma was capable of sexually sophisticated analysis. The Viennese-born writer Erwin Chargaff recalls a young journalist friend who visited Ravel for an interview at this time and was received by the composer in his room, garbed seductively in blue silk pyjamas.

Ravel was anxious to hear Schoenberg's music, but when Alma took him to a concert of Schoenberg's *Chamber Symphony,* he was "very nervous throughout the performance. 'No,' he said when we got up at the end. 'That's not music: It's from the laboratory!'" Oskar Fried, a leading disciple of Mahler, was to conduct works by Ravel during this visit, but he was a poor sight reader and begged Alma to find two pianists to play the unfamiliar scores to him. She obliged, coming up with seventeen-year-old Rudolf Serkin and the noted Schoenberg disciple Eduard Steuermann, who sat down together at Alma's piano and read their way through *Rapsodie espagnole* and *Ma Mère l'Oye.* When they had finished, Alfredo Casella took over and started improvising a fantasy on themes from Ravel's *Rapsodie,* first quietly, then louder. Ravel, who had been napping in the guest room, came in "totally frightened by the hellish din."

Alban Berg wrote to Schoenberg in October 1920, reporting on Ravel's visit and explaining that he'd worked so hard promoting the first of two concerts in homage to the visitor that he had been stricken with an asthma attack. Berg said that he'd been warned by a friend of Ravel's, Paul Clémenceau, to keep the evening short, as the Frenchman was "notorious for leaving before the end of every concert." However, despite Ravel's craving for what he called "the liberating cigarette," he did manage to hear the whole program in Vienna (another concert was programmed which he did not attend). Berg noted that in Vienna's "wealthy social circles there isn't much interest in Ravel any more than there is in us; his own two concerts were very poorly attended, despite the French embassy, etc." Ravel liked Berg's *Pieces for Clarinet and Piano, Opus 5* and brought the score back to Paris to have them performed.

Ravel's visit to Vienna also included a meeting with the poet and librettist Hugo von Hofmannsthal, at the latter's country home. Hofmannsthal's daughter Christiane noted in her journal that Ravel and a friend arrived for "many discussions and projects." Ravel might have found common ground with Hofmannsthal; both had respect for Richard Strauss's music, both adored the Spanish theater of the Golden Age, and both had worked with Diaghilev. Hofmannsthal's experience with the Ballets Russes dated back to 1912–13, when he provided the libretto for Richard Strauss's ballet *La Légende de Joseph.* He had also dreamed of a ballet libretto on *Daphnis et Chloé* before Ravel's version appeared. He told Count Harry Kessler that it could feature a "Greek-oriental slave market, that wonderful mixture found in Hellenistic times."

Ravel made friendship with Hofmannsthal difficult by disparaging Beethoven for "introducing literature into music." Hofmannsthal replied, "Really? If this is meant as anything more than a provocation . . ." and launched into a long-winded defense of Beethoven. He was so irked by Ravel's remark that he referred to it in an essay he wrote months later on the occasion of Beethoven's 150th birthday; he did not name Ravel but, with a typical mixture of aristocratic regret and resentment, made it easy for readers to identify the source: "A few weeks ago in Vienna I heard a French musician speaking, a young *Meister* whom many think is the leading representative of French music after Debussy's death." He noted Ravel's "great enthusiasm" for Mozart, but as for Beethoven—and he quoted Ravel in the original French, *"C'est Beethoven qui a introduit la littérature dans la musique."*

Ravel never changed his mind, and during another Beethoven anniversary year, 1927, he refused to subscribe to a monument to Beethoven, telling Manuel Rosenthal, "Let them build a monument to Mozart first, then we'll see. I don't see why I should contribute to a monument to the Big Deaf One."

Anecdotes are plentiful about Ravel's Ludwig-o-phobia: At a musical soirée in the late 1920s, the cellist Gregor Piatigorsky had barely finished a Beethoven program when a tiny man approached him and began talking rapid-fire French, a language the Russian did not understand. Finally Paul Painlevé came over and explained in German that the man, who had already departed, was Ravel. Piatigorsky was excited, as he had performed Ravel's duo for cello and violin with Joseph Szigeti in "pianoless" recitals in Berlin and Frankfurt, and he was proud to be the first cellist to play *Tzigane* in an arrangement for his instrument. Painlevé translated the composer's remarks about the Beethoven program: "He wanted to know why you waste your talent on such abominable music as you played tonight."

After Vienna, Ravel returned to Paris in time to see a ballet made from selected movements of his *Tombeau de Couperin,* by the Swedish ballet, and in December 1920, *La Valse* had its concert premiere. That same year, a new group of young composers made their bow and found themselves labelled by critic Henri Collet as Les Six. Darius Milhaud, Arthur Honegger, Francis Poulenc, Georges Auric, Germaine Tailleferre, and Louis Durey were friends who enjoyed socializing, although they represented different musical goals. Honegger admired Beethoven, while Poulenc and Milhaud thought Beethoven was the sort of self-consciously "serious" music that should be avoided. Where they all agreed was in drawing their inspiration from the serious but playful example of Erik Satie.

Satie's attitude toward Ravel was ironic, to say the least, and his jibe that "Ravel refuses the Legion of Honor, but all his music accepts it," became famous. Satie's wisecracks do not always reveal a precise inner meaning, but in this case he was presumably scorning the communicativeness and accessibility of much of Ravel's music, which permitted wide popularity and fame. As chief propagandist of Les Six, Cocteau was in the anti-Ravel camp, but the eldest member of the group, Louis Durey, was grateful to Ravel for his generous encouragement. Durey refused to contribute to Cocteau's project for Les Six, *Les mariés de la*

Tour Eiffel and he resigned from the group in 1921, hardly a year after Les Six had been launched, citing his colleagues' attitude toward Ravel. Honegger and Germaine Tailleferre nevertheless remained on good terms with Ravel, and Milhaud was embarrassed that he didn't admire more of his music, since the elder composer was always gracious about supporting Milhaud's work, congratulating him after concerts and speaking well of him to others.

Poulenc first went to see Ravel in the fall of 1917, bearing an introduction from Ricardo Viñes, his piano teacher. Poulenc wanted to play for him the *Sonatine* and *Le Tombeau de Couperin*, but, as usual, Ravel didn't enjoy hearing his own music performed and stopped the young man after three minutes. Quickly looking at the eighteen-year-old composer's works, Ravel praised Mendelssohn and Saint-Saëns and criticized Schumann and late Debussy, which disconcerted Poulenc. In June 1919 Poulenc wrote to Ravel's friend Georges Jean-Aubry to say how much he disliked the orchestral version of *Le Tombeau de Couperin*, finding it "cold." Over the next few years, Poulenc complained about Ravel's music, writing to friends from the 1922 Salzburg Festival to grade Ravel −11 on a scale from −20 to +20, ranking him below such composers as Karl Alwin (the husband and accompanist of the soprano Elisabeth Schumann) and Dame Ethel Smyth. Poulenc disagreed with what he saw as Ravel's aesthetic, writing to Henri Sauguet in August 1928, "You're one of the rare musicians who write with your heart; in spite of what Ravel says, we mustn't despise our loveliest organ." But his opinion of Ravel improved in 1932, when he heard his two piano concertos, while preparing his own Concerto for Two Pianos. He found the Concerto in G to be "marvellous, stuffed with music with the verve of a 30-year-old musician," which was nearly Poulenc's age when he made this remark. In 1933 he wrote to a friend that the *Concerto pour la main gauche* was "sublime," underlining the word thirteen times. Performing Ravel's songs with the baritone Pierre Bernac may have further helped Poulenc to identify with Ravel. In October 1942, he wrote to a friend that for years people had mistaken Ravel for a "small-scale master and a copier of Debussy," just as the music world saw Poulenc as a miniaturist.

Other composers' reactions differed according to whether Ravel was in the room at the moment. Sergey Prokofiev, who met him at a Paris soirée in 1920, was so servile that Ravel exclaimed, "Oh don't call me *maître*!" Yet Prokofiev, though preferring Ravel to other contemporary French composers, was often bitingly critical of his work. Aaron Copland, who studied in Paris in the 1920s, recalled that young avant-garde composers attacked Ravel because they heard in his music "little reflection of the disabused and hard new postwar world. The sensuousness and sheen of all Ravel's music, the desire to allure and disarm, the calculated brilliance and virtuosity, all seemed somehow to be part of the comfortable bourgeois world of prewar days."

Whatever Ravel's rank among young colleagues, his star in the broader world of music continued to rise. In 1921 there were revivals of *Daphnis et Chloé* and *L'Heure espagnole* at the Opéra, and he wrote *Berceuse sur le nom de Gabriel Fauré*, for violin and piano to commemorate Fauré's retirement from the Conservatoire. This *Berceuse*, or cradlesong, is a candid, private, modest, and loving evocation of an open-hearted colleague. Marked "semplice" [with simplicity], it gently rocks the listener, recalling a composer whose Requiem also provided a comforting, cossetting approach to death.

In 1922 a music publisher asked Ravel to orchestrate Debussy's *Danse* and *Sarabande,* which he gladly agreed to do. In the same year he also completed a *Sonate pour violon et violoncelle.* The work is in four movements, marked *Allegro, Tres Vif, Lent,* and *Vif, avec entrain.* It begins with rural-sounding harmonies, the drone of peasant music, with an exalted upward yearning. In the second movement, the cello's pizzicati have the freedom of jazz bass, while the violin has dramatic chords as in the later *Tzigane.* The instruments' diversity seems to contain a message about the essential incompatibility of couples. The third movement, *Lent,* is a romantic melody expressing tenderness and regret, followed by an agitated peasant dance. Ravel wanted the cello to play lively notes with a "very mechanical-rabbit" bounce of the bow. (For Ravel, pizzicati were diabolical elements.) In the finale, the cello is in the Russian folklore vein, sailing out with forte passages as if trying to call the hogs home.

One listener, the great harpsichordist Wanda Landowska, compared the "Sonate pour violon et violoncelle" to sixteenth-century French music by Gaultier Le Vieux and Louis Couperin, pointing to the "acrobatic mobility" of the two parts during which the musicians are "everywhere at once, thanks to a serpentine agility and suppleness." Violinist Hélène Jourdan-Morhange complained about the piece's difficulty, saying that Ravel expected soloists to "play the flute on the violin and the drum on the cello," and that no one would dare play such a difficult work. Ravel replied, "So much the better! That way amateurs can't bash up my music!" Since the composer couldn't be present at the first performance, given by Jourdan-Morhange and the cellist Maurice Maréchal, he jokingly suggested that she "might want to profit by my absence by playing in unison with the cello," thereby lessening the difficulties.

The *Sonate pour violon et violoncelle* is another example of what critic Charles Rosen praised as Ravel's gift for mimicry and disguise: "In his works, instruments can take on unnatural colorings and characters. The piano sounds like a guitar in *Alborada del gracioso,* and like a bell in *Le Gibet,* the cello sounds like a cat in *L'Enfant et les sortilèges* or like the ghostly rustling of ball dresses in *La Valse.* The saxophone takes on a medieval coloring in the orchestration of *Pictures at an Exhibition.*" Rosen concluded: "Part of the pleasure of listening to Ravel is hearing an instrument sound unlike itself so effortlessly, with such natural ease."

Ravel's private life continued to be disguised as well, even to close friends. An ambiguous incident from 1922 was later described by the gay composer Henri Sauguet, who recounted how at age twenty he met the elder Ravel. One day he recognized Ravel in the street, dressed with "rather affected elegance." He followed him into a bookstore and hunted through the same bin of books until the two men's hands met. Ravel asked, "I'm sorry, have you already chosen this book?" and Sauguet replied, "It's yours, *Maître,* if you want it." Ravel's face "contracted with annoyance," and he hurried out of the bookstore, hailing a taxi to escape the scene. Sauguet's overt point in this reminiscence, published in a posthumous tribute to Ravel, was that the elder man's modesty and shyness made him hate to be called "*Maître,*" but Ravel's real anxiety may have been at being recognized by a gay young musician who had cruised him.

The same year Ravel visited London for concerts, where he met the Hungarian violinist Jelly (pronounced "Yelly") d'Aranyi at a party. Robert Casadesus, also there, recalled that d'Aranyi "looked like a gypsy enveloped in a brilliant Spanish shawl, and Ravel could not take his eyes off it, enchanted with her and her music." She played gypsy melodies at Ravel's request, going on for hours. D'Aranyi was noted for her legion of lovers, including Béla Bartók, and never hesitated to seduce composers, regardless of how unlikely the object of her affection might be. Poulenc wrote in April 1922 to Milhaud about a musical soirée where d'Aranyi had gone "mad with joy" at his music, commissioned Poulenc to write her "a sonata, a concerto, etc., of which I shall never write a note, and then pinched me and said we were made to be 'friends.' She's a fiery-spirited person." Given the same sort of treatment, Ravel was musically, but not physically, stimulated. He wrote *Tzigane* for her, finishing it only a few days before its scheduled premiere in 1924, but on a personal level, d'Aranyi later declared, Ravel was "a lonely, empty-living man devoted only to his mother. . . . He believed in nothing . . . a sad pessimist."

Ravel returned to Lyons-la-forêt, home of Roland-Manuel's mother, to finish a commission from the conductor Serge Koussevitzky for an orchestration of Mussorgsky's piano work, *Pictures at an Exhibition*. Ravel went back to Mussorgsky's original piano manuscript, and found challenges in the most subtle aspects of the score, not in the slam-bang sections like the "Great Gate of Kiev" finale, which he called "the least interesting part to orchestrate." While working on the project, he was moved by the death of Pierre d'Alheim, who had first introduced Mussorgsky's music to him decades before.

Arturo Toscanini later called the Mussorgsky/Ravel *Pictures* a "textbook in orchestration," but this work has been looked down upon by some, such as the author of *The BBC Guide to Ravel's Orchestral Music*, who called it "very superior hackwork." The BBC author further compared the section "Samuel Goldenberg and Schmuyle" to "the American-Semitic parables with which we are nowadays beset . . . the phraseology of the Bellows and the Malamuds."

In 1923 Ravel sketched out a violin sonata (with piano this time) and completed a song, *Ronsard à son âme*, on the occasion of that poet's four-hundredth birthday. He wrote to Manuel de Falla in January, 1924: "Depression made me abandon my Sonata, perhaps momentarily. . . . while waiting, I've managed to write my 'Epitaph,' or at least Ronsard's, and I put as much spirit into it as if it were for myself." This dream-song of death has the chaste harmonies of early music, explaining how the soul goes to the kingdom of the dead, with an acceptance of the inevitability of death. The song's piano accompaniment is mostly for the right hand alone, and Ravel said that it was his favorite song because he could perform it while holding a cigarette in one hand while he accompanied with the other.

Ravel wrote an apologetic letter to Hélène Joudan-Morhange in March 1924, excusing himself for putting aside the "damned" violin sonata intended for her, in order to write *Tzigane*. His excuse was that it wouldn't have been "chic" to have invited d'Aranyi to play anything less than a major new showpiece and, to further ward off jealousies, said that d'Aranyi would have a mere couple of days to master the wicked difficulties of the new score. But by the time he did finish his violin sonata, Jourdan-Morhange had retired from performing due to finger problems.

Ravel's music publisher, Jacques Durand, recalled that when the composer tried to show him the newly finished *Tzigane* in 1924, he played the violin and piano parts simultaneously on the piano, but the result, hampered by Ravel's poor technique, gave Durand little idea what he was driving at. He asked two young American musicians, the violinist Samuel Dushkin and the pianist Beveridge Webster, to play through the work at a private hearing.

When Bohuslav Martinu was asked to describe the special characteristics of his violin concerto, he replied in one word: "Violin." The same can be said about *Tzigane,* the apotheosis of the diabolic for an instrument that was attributed supernatural powers from the days of Paganini, taken by some audiences to be the devil himself, and of Tartini's "Devil's Trill" Sonata. *Tzigane* is the concentrated essence of what the romantic violin expressed through Sarasate, incorporating Hungarian rhapsodies by Liszt and Brahms. It requires an apotheosis of a fiddler, like the young Jascha Heifetz or Ginette Neveu. Like Donizetti's writing for coloratura soprano in mad scenes, Ravel embraced the bizarre qualities of virtuoso violin technique. The violin repertoire is full of pieces with titles involving elves, gremlins, and goblins. Ravel returned to these magic sources in *Tzigane,* where even a bit of Mendelssohnian fairy music is audible in the final accelerando. Throughout, the piano part of French elegance complements the manic fiddle.

During a concert tour to Spain at this time, Ravel met his sometime student, the openly gay music historian Adolfo Salazar. He rehearsed an orchestra in Madrid, using "the few words of

Spanish, Italian, and nigger that I manage to put together." Ravel told Salazar that his music derived from Charles Gounod's opera *Mireille* and Satie, which shocked the student considerably.

Satie was indeed still an influence. When the composer of *Socrate* declared in an interview in March 1924, "I came into the world very young at a very old time," Ravel was quick to paraphrase this in a letter to a friend: "I came too young into a generation too old." He was referring to conservative critics and composers who stymied advanced thinkers.

One of Ravel's most advanced projects became his second and last opera, *L'Enfant et les sortilèges,* begun before World War I, when the director of the Opéra, Jacques Rouché, asked Colette for a libretto for a dance called a *féerie-ballet.* Colette churned out a libretto in less than a week, and when Rouché went over a list of composers who might set the fairy play to music, she chose Ravel immediately. He accepted, no doubt seduced by the enchanted and childlike story. However, the composer was as slow as Colette had been rapid, and *L'Enfant* was not finished until more than five years later, when Ravel was solicited by the director of the Monte Carlo Opéra, Raoul de Gunsbourg, who wanted to stage a new work. By then, Colette noted, she'd had hardly any contact with Ravel for years. Diaghilev necessarily became part of the creative team insofar as he had a contract to provide the dance spectacles at the Monte Carlo Opéra. Otherwise, it is unlikely that Ravel would have chosen to work with him again so soon after *La Valse.*

Working feverishly to finish *L'Enfant et les sortilèges,* Ravel joked with Hélène Casella in June, "I've promised to finish a job so considerable that I'll be forced to ask for the help of Milhaud," who was known for his prolific ease in composition.

The title *L'Enfant et les Sortilèges* has been variously translated as The Dreams of a Naughty Boy, The Child and the Sorceries, or, as Virgil Thomson suggested, Childhood Hallucinations. It is a fairy tale, an evocation of childhood fantasy with a near-miraculous orchestral sophistication. The opera begins with a child onstage, a role which Ravel intended to be sung by a woman. A woman portraying a child implied conscious artistry. Staged "realistically" with a child singer, the rapport with the mother becomes problematic, as a twelve-year-old boy singing the role is too grown-up for it. The anthropologist Claude Lévi-Strauss, presumably with this sort of staging in mind, claimed that in *L'Enfant*, Ravel "allowed himself to be trapped by a libretto that is intellectually low and morally indefensible . . . a libretto in which the author odiously staged her own apotheosis as Castrating Mother . . . with the Child, whom she calls Baby, even though he is of school age."

Lévi-Strauss's image of a castrating mother is reasonable: the mother appears onstage (or her lower half, all that is visible according to the stage directions) with a pair of scissors dangling from her waist, evoking the Scissors Man from *Struwwelpeter* who cuts off thumbs of naughty boys. Yet the mother's concern about the boy's behavior is also shown to be justified when he is seized by a "frenzy of perversity." Attacking animals and wreaking havoc on the scenery, the child cries, "I am free, free, wicked and free!" The boy yanks out a grandfather clock's pendulum, the same symbolic act of emasculation as in *L'Heure espagnole*. The child's gender was originally a point of discord between the composer and librettist. Colette called her first sketch for the libretto, *Ballet for My Daughter,* which Ravel rejected, saying, "I haven't got a daughter." He didn't have a son, either, but the child became a boy, for the purpose of self-identification.

Exhausted, the naughty boy falls into a large armchair that comes alive and dances with a Louis XV-style wing chair. In the piano score for *L'Enfant,* a duo between teapot and cup in mock-English conversation lacked the text for the first few notes composed by Ravel. Some words were added later in a different hand, a curvaceous script that also added tempo indications in Italian to the score. The first question of the teapot to the cup, "How's your mug?" involves a pun that outclassed Ravel's knowledge of English, and the addition may have been written by Victor de Sabata, the young Italian music director of the Monte Carlo Opéra who led the premiere.

A boxer enters, singing with a distinct sexual slant, "Black, black, black and thick and really handsome kid, and really handsome kid." Ravel spent many nights watching black musicians and dancers in Paris nightclubs, and at Le Boeuf sur le Toit he would have seen Cocteau with his black American lover, a drug-addicted boxer named Al Brown.

English-speaking blacks were a means of expressing erotic sentiments, as were Asians, in the "nonsense" language spouted by the China cup. The phrase "Kekta Foutu d'mon Ka-oud" may be read as "Qu'est-ce que tu as foutu de mon . . . ?" [What the fuck have you done with my . . . ?] The phonetic spelling in this part of the libretto may be linked to French surrealism, like Raymond Queneau's spellings of Parisian slang in his novel *Zazie dans le métro* or Marcel Duchamp's code message "Elle a chaud au cul" [She Has a Hot Arse], concealed in the caption "L.H.O.O.Q." beneath the bearded Mona Lisa.

L'Enfant's concealments and codes include mention of "Sessue Hayakawa," a Japanese silent screen star who was the first Asian man to play a romantic role in a western film, *The Cheat*. Eroticized black and Asian men are part of the hallucinatory scene of household objects coming to life. Exotic male sexuality was meant to disturb the audience of Ravel's opera as much as it baffles the child.

Fire appears, to make explicit the underlying Greek superstition in the libretto, that the child has offended the household gods, who "held back the fragile barrier between you and bad luck." Although fire, *le feu*, is masculine in gender, the role is for a hysterical coloratura soprano who is in turn extinguished after a dance with ashes (*les cendres*). A princess arrives, saying that her story, begun yesterday, "kept you awake so long." On the piano score of the opera, Ravel substituted the word *éveillé* [awake] for another word, now illegible, perhaps in a reference to his own insomnia and the nightlong story-telling of Shéhérazade. The princess asks, "Do we know how long a dream lasts?" and when she is pulled back into earth by Sleep and Night, the child tries in vain to hold on to her. The fairy tale aspect of her short aria *Toi, le coeur de la rose*, is exquisitely moving in its combination of tender innocence and graceful beauty. Indeed, the composer who wrote this remained in some ways in an exalted state of childhood his whole life long, as many of his friends suggested.

131

An old man/mathematician enters, singing of a "paysanne, zanne, zanne, zanne," in a music-hall style that would later influence Poulenc's *Le Bal Masqué,* which features a "paysan de Chine, chine, chine." Ravel's mathematician screams out sums with a frenzy that only someone from a family of engineers could express. Violins and cellos—catgut instruments—evoke giant cats, and one orchestral effect is labeled "cat spit." A tree frog's stuttered "ca-ca-ca-cage" is a juvenile joke about a "shitty cage" in French. The most personal reference is to the large liquid eyes of a squirrel, who longs for "the free sky, the free wind, my free brothers, leaping confidently as if they were flying." Several of Ravel's friends, including Colette, said he resembled a squirrel. Animals terrifyingly attack the child, but he is rescued because he displays a technical skill that the animals lack, bandaging the paw of the wounded squirrel.

To save him, the animals resort to imitation, aping the boy's cry for "Maman!" The child's final apotheosis is haloed in moonlight as the chorus sings, "He is good. . . . He is well-behaved." Like the song *Le Noël des jouets,* it is a Christian scene in which the worm of evil has already intruded. Ravel gave as dateline for the score, "Different places, 1920–25," and those places included his garden at Montfort l'Amaury, "palpitating with wings . . . a paradise of tenderness."

In Monte Carlo for the opening of *L'Enfant et les sortilèges,* Ravel ran into Diaghilev in a hotel lobby. The snub over *La Valse* still hurt, because when Diaghilev held out his hand, Ravel refused to shake it, challenging him to a duel. Serge Lifar, who recalled the incident, noted that Diaghilev "was hardly used to this, as he was always forgiven everything." The duel didn't take place, but Lifar remembered "the painful moments Diaghilev went through at the time." This was not the only duel bruited about during the first performances. The critic Jean Marnold also challenged Opéra Comique director Jacques Rouché to a duel, ostensibly because Rouché had delayed staging Ravel's opera, but this duel never happened either.

The choreographer for *L'Enfant et les sortilèges* was twenty-year-old George Balanchine, in his first major job for the Ballets Russes. Balanchine spoke no French, and Ravel only a few Russian curses, but the composer indicated his tempos at the piano, while the choreographer stood by, his face twitching with the nervous tic that won him the nickname Rat at ballet school. Diaghilev threatened to withdraw his dancers from the production, supposedly because the music was too complicated and available too late. But the production supervisor, René Léon, observed drily, "It's really odd that these difficulties only became apparent a few hours after an incident you apparently had with Ravel in the Hôtel de Paris lobby, after which several witnesses heard you say, 'I will never let them dance in his opera.'"

Léon threatened not to renew his contract with Diaghilev, who capitulated, and the dancers appeared as scheduled. Still, after the premiere, half of the ten dancers who worked in the production did not show up one evening, making further threats necessary. The break between Diaghilev and Ravel was final, but before he died in 1929, Diaghilev complained that without Ravel to write ballets for him, his commissions resulted in *musiquettes* [itsy-bitsy music].

Reviews of *L'Enfant* were rhapsodic, with few dissenters. Prokofiev was of two minds. After the premiere, he wrote to

Serge Koussevitzsky, "The orchestration is heavenly, he has devised many charming tricks, but as is often the case with Ravel, the music lacks substance." Ravel was at work again immediately on a new commission from Elisabeth Sprague Coolidge, an American who, although deaf, was an avid sponsor of new chamber music. The conductor and cellist Hans Kindler, who had played the "Sonate pour violon et violoncelle" with Jelly d'Aranyi in a London salon, asked on behalf of Mrs. Coolidge for a song cycle with accompaniment of flute, cello, and piano, "if possible," and the result would be *Trois Chansons madécasses*.

Ravel's fiftieth birthday was celebrated in 1925 with a special issue of *La Revue musicale* in which friends and colleagues wrote flattering tributes. Reacting to this milestone, Ravel toyed with the idea of producing two books, one about orchestration, which he planned to illustrate with examples of bad orchestration taken from his own works. The second was to be a memoir of Claude Debussy. Recognizing that he had no patience to sit and write lengthy texts, he requested as amanuensis Georges Auric, who had already typed *Le Bal du Comte d'Orgel*, the novel by Cocteau's lover, Raymond Radiguet. Auric agreed, but the books were never even begun.

Ravel's choice of the *Chansons madécasses* hearkened back to his student years with Ricardo Viñes, who had introduced him to the work of Evariste Parny. He was aware of the music of Madegascar at least since 1900, when his friend Louis Benedictus published a book of melodies, *"Les Musiques bizarres à l'Exposition de 1900: Les Chants de Madagascar,"* which he had transcribed at the Exposition Universelle. The "Madegascar Songs'" of "tender Parny," as Pushkin called him, written in 1787 in India, really have nothing to do with Madagascar. Like Klingsor's poems for *Shéhérazade,* they express a desire to flee the constraints of Western social structure. The first song, in praise of the charms of a lovely girl, Nahandove, begins with the drone of the cello, in a folklore vein. The second song, *Aoua,* begins with a shout, like a Polynesian chieftain's roar across a mountaintop. The message is, "Beware of whites, who make promises but take them back." Monumental piano and vocal parts, with mournful cello accompaniment, express white oppression of the native peoples: "Their priests wanted to give us a God that we don't know." The priests "were all exterminated" for their pains. With choked emotion, a profoundly pagan sentiment emerges, in contrast to the natives' exultant "And we live free." At the premiere, a French version of Colonel Blimp stalked out of the theater, complaining that he would not listen to such things when France was embroiled in a colonial struggle in Morocco.

In the third song, after love and death, comes sleep. The high notes of the flute, cello, and piano, combine to evoke native pipe-playing. The message is, "The dance is for me almost as sweet as a kiss." The song ends with the unaccompanied command, "Go and prepare the meal."

As this cycle might suggest, Ravel felt sympathy for artistic aspirations of black people, although in letters he referred to them as "*nègres,*" as did most white Parisians of the time. In the early to mid-1920s Parisian nightclubbers, including Ravel, went to the Théâtre des Champs-Elysées to hear Josephine Baker, to the restaurant Les Ambassadeurs to hear Florence Mills and her Blackbirds, and to Bricktop's nightclub, where Duke Ellington's pieces were played.

But Ravel's favorite hangout was Le Boeuf sur le Toit, where the European piano duo Jean Wiéner and Clément Doucet held court, mixing Mozart with ragtime. The Polish actress Dagmar Godowsky recalled a night when the pianist Arthur Rubinstein took her there, and Ravel proudly showed her photos of his beloved Siamese cats. The nightclub offered Ravel company, cocktails which he loved, and a view of androgynous people. As Victor Seroff reported, "It was hard to tell the male and female 'Boeuf sur le toit' habitués apart, so mannish were the suits of the women and so baggy the trousers of the men." According to friends, Ravel was fascinated by the young gay men at Le Boeuf sur le Toit, who danced with one another, although he never danced himself. He also frequented Le Monocle, a lesbian bar, and Le Dingo, a rendezvous for gays and lesbians, where he would usually sit alone. He would also go with his friend Jacques de Zogheb to a venerable whorehouse, Le Sphinx, where he would talk with the prostitutes while his friend employed their services.

At this time Ravel also thought about writing an operetta with the variety singer Maud Loty as star. The project never came to fruition, but he wrote to Roland-Manuel in July 1925: "I'm not doing a fucking thing, but I may perhaps fuck an operetta. All my time is dedicated to vegetating and keeping an eye on the fantasies of Jazz (the dog) who knows an infinite number of tricks." He told another friend about Jazz, who "tears my clothes, rips out flowers, mistakes his gruel for a footbath, makes holes in the garden, leaves droppings wherever he likes, and runs to his house only when he sees the whip. We didn't do all that when *we* were two months old."

CHAPTER SIX

Indian Summer

1926–1932

Ravel spent a good part of 1926 working on his *Sonate pour violon et piano,* and giving lessons to Manuel Rosenthal, a composer who would become a close friend and colleague, like Roland-Manuel and Maurice Delage. Together they made up what Ravel humorously called the "School of Montfort." Ravel's relationship with Rosenthal, as with other students, had something of a mother-child rapport; the master was often exaggeratedly strict, tearing up a student's work, followed by tears from the pupil, and apologies by the master. On occasion, Ravel would decide he had had enough of a pupil and declare, "Now hate me." Other students, like Rosenthal, Delage, and Roland-Manuel, he cherished for the rest of his life, despite their different lifestyles and habits. Delage and his wife, Louis Laloy, Georges Auric, and Paul Morand were opium smokers in the 1920s, but when they offered a puff to Ravel, he would refuse, saying that it didn't do anything for him: "I don't feel the need," he would claim.

He did feel the need to dabble in erotica, however. His collection of pornography was disposed of by his brother, Edouard, before the house at Montfort-l'Amaury became a national museum, and among the documents destroyed was a notebook called "My Atrocities," a mock response to charges of German atrocities during the war. Rosenthal recalled that "My Atrocities" contained Ravel's plan for the moment when the conquering French soldiers marched into Berlin in 1918. He wanted the young Frenchmen to wait until lovely Berlin girls came to their balconies to admire them, when an order would be given for the soldiers to "open their flies" at the count of one, and on the count of two, shout in unison, "You're not getting any of this!"

Ravel's fantasy of soldiers with their flies undone en masse recalls the military-garbed erotica drawn by gay artists like Charles Demuth and Tom of Finland. Added to mass phallic exposure is the element of sexual exhibitionism in measured time, as both a musical and mechanical ordering of sex. Denying the phallus to women, in public and collectively, is also part of the schoolboy joke. And the balcony as a place for erotic voyeurism dated back to his childhood, when he would look over the place de Clichy with Ricardo Viñes.

Along with Rosenthal, Ravel had another composition pupil, Nicolas Obouhov, who had "a strong muscular body and made a living in Paris as a bricklayer," according to Nicolas Slonimsky. Obouhov, who came to Paris after the Russian Revolution, was a religious fanatic who used to sign his name as "Nicholas the Illuminated One." His major work was a two- thousand-page choral "Book of Life," with passages of the score written in his own blood, "symbolic of Christ's martyrdom," and vocal parts that included screaming, shouting, sighing, and groaning. Obouhov also invented an electronic instrument called the Sonic Cross, composing works for it.

In Obouhov's imposing physicality and wildness, Ravel may have been trying to reexperience the Russian insanity he had known with Nijinsky. The Dyonisian strain in Obouhov's ravings corresponded to Ravel's need for the demonic in art, the possessed and magical. Ravel was so diverted by the unleashed Slavic temperament that he even put up with it in his unruly Czech maidservant, Prohaska. He gave Obouhov financial support and letters of recommendation, and he convinced the conductor Serge Koussevitzky to perform excerpts from "Book of Life" at a Paris concert in 1926. At the performance the two piano parts were played by Obouhov and Nicolas Slonimsky, and a friend suggested that Slonimsky wear a placard, *"Je ne suis pas le compositeur"* [I am not the composer] because the program did not specify which pianist wrote the work and he wouldn't want to be blamed. Koussevitzky apologized in rehearsal for performing such an awful work but protested that Ravel had claimed Obouhov was a genius.

Ravel was drawn to failures. His friend Georges Jean-Aubry, the Joseph Conrad specialist, had given him many of Conrad's books, and when Rosenthal commented that the stories were always about failures, Ravel looked at him and replied, "Naturally." In a success story there was no artistic potential.

A sometime pupil in the 1920s was the British composer Lennox Berkeley, who was puzzled by the barriers Ravel put up against human relations: "He was never known to have any intimate relationship with either woman or man, and this is curious when one considers the extreme tenderness and often passionate feeling in his music. Whether it was that his real tastes were in contradiction with his ethical standards, or that he feared any loss of that great self-control and poise, no one will ever know."

Others also had their suspicions about his real tastes. The cellist Gérard Hekking, who went on concert tours through Europe with Ravel and was himself known to be gay, said that after their performances the two musicians would change their clothes and Ravel, chain-smoking, would stalk the streets of strange cities until four A.M. or later, favoring "the life of the docks at seaports." Part of that life was sailor's bars, a notorious place for gay men to find companionship in strange cities. Had Ravel wished to indulge himself, he could have have done so in anonymity and none of his friends would have been the wiser.

In September 1926 Ravel wrote to Roland-Manuel, "Everything is fairly well here. My governess [the composer's term for his housekeeper] twisted her foot, one of my little Siamese cats, the most energetic one who stuffed himself like a piglet, has got gastritis and his master is starved by cerebral anemia or senility. To you and yours, if you're still in Dieppe, the most affectionate of my last lucid thoughts."

Ravel often made half-comic allusions to his senility or cerebral problems, which in retrospect take on a tragic cast. When not composing, he enjoyed gravitating in high political circles, relishing the contact with power after his failure to sway government opinion in the only cause he ever embraced, Liabeuf's. He wrote to a friend in 1926 about a forthcoming party at the French Ministry of Finance, "where I will rescue the franc." He demanded a certain standard of behavior even from politicians and refused to see Paul Painlevé socially after he had lied to Ravel by denying that he was a member of the Masonic guild.

Ravel's *Sonate pour Violin et Piano* was completed in 1927, after about five years of work. The piece was actually Ravel's second for the two instruments, if his youthful sonata is taken into account. Some listeners have heard in the French composer's score the influence of Bartok's violin sonatas from 1921 and 1922. But Ravel's sonata, his last chamber work, was very much his own. The musical lines for the violin and piano are strongly independent of one another. Although the sonata is in the traditional three movements, the highly developed first movement, *Allegretto,* containing four separate themes, is followed by an unconventional *Blues* movement and a *Perpetuum Mobile Allegro.*

The first movement begins in a pastoral, even barnyard style. The fiddle and piano change quickly to a rhapsodic melody of crystalline clarity. The violin's high notes have a sad, pure, solitary tone. In the slow second movement, the violin sounds at times like a banjo, and even a saxophone. The *Blues* movement in particular retains a fresh, improvisatory feel, with plucking and stroking, as much "Turkey in the Straw" as African-American jazz. The blues referred to is really ragtime, early New Orleans–Chicago style, bawdy-house dance tunes with the sassiness of a prewar cakewalk. Ravel was not transcribing the latest jazz sounds as heard in Bricktop's club. The end of the movement drives forward like a ragtime funeral, with a comical postlude tacked on, "and that ain't all." Ravel used traditions of African-American music with love but not excessive respect.

The final movement goes back to barnyard pecking, and it is unclear what this finale has to do with the jazz spoof that preceded it. There is something of Rimsky-Korsakov's *Flight of the Bumblebee* in the rapid *Perpetuum Mobile* that rounds off the score with a final brief remembrance of the closing chords of Ravel's Quartet, written decades before. The sonata's whole sequence evokes the urban confusion of modern times, a night spent on the town in Paris, first in a bar, then in the traffic on the Champs-Elysées.

The work was completed too late for its intended recipient, Jourdan-Morhange, who was sidelined from playing by finger problems. Uncharacteristically, Ravel hinted to a few friends that he had proposed marriage to Jordan-Morhange, but it seems highly improbable that there was any romantic affair between them. At the time Jordan-Morhange was living with the artist Luc-Albert Moreau, and she rejected the proposal—if indeed it occurred. She made no mention of it in her own numerous writings about Ravel.

Instead, the *Sonate pour Violon et Piano* was first performed by Georges Enesco and Ravel, but the Romanian violinist disliked the *Blues* central movement and didn't even stay for the ritual drink with the composer after the concert. In 1932 Vienna, after Szigeti performed the *Blues* movement, Nazis in the audience screamed "Nigger music! Phooey!" Others were inspired by the *Blues* movement. Bartók confessed to Szigeti that the opening of his own work *Contrasts* for violin, piano, and clarinet was inspired by the pizzicato start of the *Blues* movement, which Szigeti and Bartók often performed together in recitals. Being indebted to Ravel did not bother Bartók in the least.

After finishing the sonata Ravel dashed off a brief *Fanfare* as a thank-you to a Paris hostess, Jeanne Dubost, who held a popular arts salon. This was the opening number of a playful ballet, *L'Eventail de Jeanne,* with contributions by Ravel, Ibert, Roussel,

Poulenc, Auric, and others, conducted in the Dubost apartment by Roger Désormière. *Fanfare* is a mock-Wagnerian pastiche, with a drumroll, peeping of fifes, and noble brass that mutates into "Taps" played sharp, with string pizzicati in a Spanish rhythm before a final cymbal crash. Paris Opéra director Jacques Rouché wanted the work performed at the Opéra in 1929, which irked Milhaud, who did not want his Opéra début to be a trivial polka. Despite such larking, Ravel sometimes looked preoccupied at the Dubost salon, as the violinist Nathan Milstein recalled: "He was sitting apart from the other guests, his face buried in his collar, only his big nose showing. Almost no one approached him, he was so forbidding. He seemed to have come from the pages of my favorite writer, Anton Chekhov. A typical Chekhovian character."

In February 1927, responding to a commission from the magazine *Les Feuilles libres* in honor of Léon-Paul Fargue, Ravel wrote a setting of Fargue's poem "Rêves." With music as transparent and unpretentious as the words, he evoked childhood, the "brief things that die wise," in solidarity with Fargue as an adult who had attained childlike wisdom. Ravel did not slow down his schedule, although he appeared older. A portrait drawn by Luc-Albert Morcau in 1927 shows him wearing thick-framed spectacles, which he was too vain to wear when being photographed.

Around this time Léon-Paul Fargue introduced him to a young friend, André Beucler, waking the latter at 3 A.M. to come to a bar to meet the composer. Beucler saw in Ravel the "slightly dry, severe face of a marine officer, or a loner like Alain Gerbault," who wanted to "flee those like him." (Gerbault, a lean, bronzed sailor who made grueling solo journeys, was often featured in the French press.)

That night Ravel was wearing a suit "the deep gray color of cold caviar, a very pale pink shirt whose collar was slightly pinched by a butterfly-knot tie. Even seated, he looked rather little, concentrated, furious but proud, and there's no other word, distinguished. Fargue and Ravel gave each other tender little pokes." The two old friends recalled that they'd first met in the home of Maurice Delage in 1902 at a time when, bearded, they "resembled each other." When a bore appeared and asked to be introduced, Fargue presented Ravel to him as "Emile Tavan," explaining to other bar patrons that the composer was "going through a brief Stendhalian period," meaning that he was using aliases as the novelist had. Right from the *Apache* days, when he used the fictitious "Gomez de Riquet" as a social excuse, bunburying, as in Wilde's *Importance of Being Earnest,* was a time-honored habit.

That evening, Fargue went back to a long-discussed but never-realized project with Ravel, for a ballet, *Les Violins de Paris,* in which popular songs were to be treated as authentic folk music. During a later visit to the Passage de l'Industrie, Paris's version of Tin Pan Alley, Ravel pointed to photos of popular singers and said that they were the real bards of their time. Decades later, the pianist Paul Crossley discovered that Ravel may have possibly composed a famous slow waltz, *Fascination,* for the popular singer Paulette Darty, but concealed his authorship by having it attributed to its publisher, Marchetti. Satie and many other composers dabbled in popular music, but few with Ravel's combination of success and secrecy.

In November 1927 Ravel suggested a program to Roland-Manuel for an ISCM festival in Siena the following year, which shows his musical interests of the moment: on his list were Pierné's *Chamber Sonata,* Rosenthal's *Sinfonietta,* Delage's *Haikaïs,* Obouhov's *Amour* for large orchestra, and a string quartet by the French composer Jean Cartan, who would die at age twenty-five in 1932. Apart from the conductor Pierné, all the composers he hoped to advance were young and struggling. He typically showed delicacy with younger talents. As the only juror at a music prize to vote for Germaine Tailleferre, he decided not to write to tell her that she'd lost because his monogrammed envelope "would give her a false hope."

Meanwhile, he had still not solved his financial problems, so that when he was offered a lucrative tour of America he accepted, although it was a long, tiring program. He went on an alcohol-free diet before leaving for Prohibition-era America and grumped to Louise Alvar: "I'm as burdened as can be, to the point where the cook, touched by the severity of my diet, added a bit of milk to my morning tapioca." He hoped to see Alvar before leaving "or else we'll see each other in the other world," a hint that he saw the crossing to the New World as a kind of symbolic death.

He went back to drinking after being assured that there would be a full supply of French wines made available to him during the tour, Prohibition or no. Even more important, his Caporal cigarettes, without which he was unable to function, were sent across the ocean. When Ravel arrived in his New York hotel room, his first question was, "Are my cigarettes here?" After paying an eighteen-dollar import tax, he was delighted to be handed a "huge package of imported cigarettes," according to an American journalist who witnessed the scene. Asked about Prohibition, he answered somewhat ambiguously, "Prohibition? Well, it's all right, but I haven't seen much of it. I can get along with Prohibition because there isn't any such thing, but if they take away my cigarettes I'll stay in France. Have you got a match, please?"

Mrs. Elie Robert Schmitz, whose husband had organized the tour and guaranteed Ravel a minimum return of ten thousand dollars, unpacked the maestro's clothes, later reporting: "Twenty pairs of pyjamas, dozens of gay shirts and waistcoats, ties galore—Maurice Ravel's trousseau was something to shout about!" Ravel was "in a state" because his new evening ties, delivered just before he sailed, were a half-inch too long, so Mrs. Schmitz shortened them—all fifty-seven of them. In New York he strolled the streets in the evening wearing a short yellow overcoat, a big white woolen muffler, and white wool gloves. According to witnesses, he "stopped traffic" in this garb. His dandyism only increased with the years. Once he refused to go onstage to conduct because he'd lost his monogrammed handkerchief, and he refused to accept the soloist Robert Casadesus's because it had the tiny initials "RC" embroidered on it, instead of his own. He was taken to Harlem nightclubs like Connie's Inn, and George Gershwin took him to the Savoy Ballroom, where Ravel wanted to know why cigarettes in glasses on the table were called "grass," not understanding the slang term for marijuana: "Pourquoi appelle-t-on ça 'grrrrasse'?"

The four-month tour was a great success, if a time-consuming one. He traveled to two dozen cities in the United States and Canada and conducted, among others, the orchestras in New York, San Francisco, Chicago, Cleveland, and Boston. Typically he conducted with a score, not from memory, and stuck rigidly to his own ideas for tempos, even when they struck some musicians as being too slow. His mechanized movements managed nevertheless to give orchestras an idea of what he wanted to hear in his own music, and he conducted no one else's during the tour. He crossed the USA five times, with New York as a starting point, to the west, north, and south. Getting used to the American audience's habit of standing ovations and whistling approval—in Paris, whistling is considered an insult—he seemed to thrive on the physical demands of the tour. As an insomniac he found it restful to take train rides with enforced hours for sleep, instead of roaming city streets, which was how he often spent his nights in Europe.

On January 15 he played a début recital in New York's Gallo Theater, accompanying Joseph Szigeti in his Violin Sonata. Szigeti later described Ravel's "unconcerned" style of piano playing and his acceptance of his own limits as a pianist, secure in the knowledge that the work existed in printed form whatever a given performance might sound like. This was a change for Szigeti after his performances with Béla Bartók, a mighty pianist who loved rehearsing. Since rehearsing with Ravel would not greatly improve the performance, the Frenchman and Szigeti chatted instead, the latter admiring the "intensely illuminating critical flashes in Ravel's conversation."

During their chats, Ravel trotted out his ideas about Hungarian music, "about Liszt, the unjustly underrated composer and trailblazer; about his indebtedness to Liszt in his piano writing; then about that Hungarian instrument, the cimbalom, and the conversation naturally drifted to *Tzigane,* which Ravel had lately composed for my compatriot and former classmate Yelly d'Aranyi," Szigeti later wrote.

By mentioning the cimbalom, whose sound he had in mind when writing the piano part of *Tzigane,* Ravel was preparing to

147

ask Szigeti if he would perform the work. But Szigeti, whose serious violin recitals featured Brahms and Beethoven, detested *Tzigane*, the apotheosis of violinistic glitz: "I suppose my being Hungarian has something to do with it, but I have never been able to overcome the resistance I always felt and still feel toward this brilliant and (to my mind) synthetically produced pastiche of Ravel's." Ravel changed the subject from *Tzigane* without Szigeti having to voice disapproval: "He must have sensed this, for I distinctly remember that his conversation swerved suddenly to Edgar Allan Poe's elaborate description of the genesis of *The Raven*. Then . . . taking Poe's essay as starting point, he expounded some of his pet theories of conscious cerebration, which insure the mechanical excellence of whatever a composer sets out to do, in however remote a field, whatever idiom he chooses to write in."

Ravel was in fact offering an oblique defense of *Tzigane*'s qualities. The fiddler commented, "My somewhat chauvinistic 'hands-off' attitude when it came to Hungarian folklore may have nettled him, and may, too, have been the reason for the otherwise reticent master's going into such detailed theorizing. It was later that I learned how partial he was to accepting the challenge of folklore in his work." Years later, Szigeti recalled his talk with the composer as being "better than the concert."

The Gallo Theater was sold out, with seat prices ranging up to five dollars, a considerable sum in those days. *Musical America* described the crush: "People packed the stage, which was distracting to everyone, and not the least so to Mr. Ravel himself, and they stood up or even sat down on the floor at the back of the house, which was a little too conducive to irrelevant conversations." Milton Blackstone, a violist who performed in Ravel's

Quartet on January 15, said that Ravel didn't look like a composer, but "a financier with artistic tendencies, or perhaps a successful lawyer, as his piercing eyes seem to look right through you." On the night of the New York concert, Blackstone found that Ravel "was not excited or impatient. [The musicians were] on tiptoes, but it seemed to mean nothing but a big party to Ravel. Judging by the way he acted, we might have been gathered at his home in France. Behind the scenes he was a perfect host, when in reality he was the guest of all those hundreds of people in the theatre."

Onstage, Ravel was described by one critic as a "fidgety little man seated at a piano, struggling with the notes of a composition long since submerged in his consciousness." Samuel Chotzinoff wrote in the *New York World* on February 27, "Mr. Ravel showed almost too much of the detached pedantic composer in his concert yesterday. His playing was polished, infinitely whimsical, yet remote and preoccupied, as though he were gazing with wonder upon what he had done and puzzling vaguely whether he could ever do it again."

The *New York Evening World* critic was exasperated to see the French harpist Carlos Salzedo, a fine pianist, turning the pages for Ravel, and cracked that the music would have "fared better if Mr. Salzedo had played the piano and Mr Ravel had turned the pages." When Ravel reached Chicago, the *Musical Courrier* wrote, "Ravel has won Chicago. . . . He has sown the seed of his own inspiration in the musical fields of Illinois." But another local critic, named Gunn, grumbled, "Only a supreme ironist would consent to play his own beautiful music in public as badly as Ravel plays it. He plays even worse than Johannes Brahms did in his declining years, and Brahms set a mark for all bad pianists to shoot at. However, it is a tradition that composers play badly, and no one can complain that Ravel does not respect it."

Ravel snatched some time for tourism, visiting Niagara Falls and the home of Edgar Allan Poe. He also saw the Grand Canyon, writing home to Roland-Manuel's family: "The seventeenth century itself would have loved these mountains, which are more like gigantic, harmonious constructions. And this splendid 'Painted Desert,' where the plesiosaurus and pterodactyls left traces of their footsteps!"

Back in Boston, the *Evening Transcript* critic scrutinized Ravel's conducting technique: "He swings a longish stick . . . frugal of movement, unfailingly clear and precise . . . a narrow arc. Of his left hand he makes little use: oftenest, it lifts an admonitory forefinger, upturned or outthrust when it would emphasize a salient detail, or assure a vivid transition. Mr. Ravel's body moves more conspicuously than his arms, bending eagerly forward when he would gain a sweep of tone, relaxing at the knees and stooping when he would impose other unities and ardors."

An American soprano, Lisa Roma, was selected as vocalist by the tour's sponsor, but she was criticized for reading from the score at concerts and singing off-key, and she dropped out halfway through the tour. Ravel's friend Eva Gauthier wrote that the musicians assigned to him "were not competent to interpret his works—vocalists could not speak French—and there was an unpleasant lawsuit with one of the singers."

In February, en route to Omaha, Ravel wrote to his brother, misspelling the town's name, saying that he'd soon be in "Ohama" and that "jazz in Ohama is famous." His worries about Prohibition were ill-founded: In Cleveland he wrote home about "good wines and great cognac," whereas in New Orleans his meal was "washed down with French wines (But yes! If you only knew what Prohibition means!)"

In Cleveland he was presented to a student musician, David Diamond. At thirteen years old, Diamond was an appealing young violinist and composer with carrot-red hair who spoke some French. When they first met after a performance, Ravel wore a tailcoat, and Diamond still recalls the sharp planes in his face, like the sculpted portrait by Léon Leyritz, and the fact that at thirteen he himself was already slightly taller than the composer. Ravel stared at Diamond, then smiled and exclaimed, "It's *Poil de Carotte!*"—a reference to the scampish redheaded hero of the novel and play by Jules Renard. Ravel took hold of Diamond's purple turtleneck sweater and felt it, saying *"très beau,"* and flicked his fingers through Diamond's hair. Then abruptly, he said, "So, the music!" Looking at Diamond's early composition efforts, he clucked *"Oh Oh Oh, ça alors!"* like a bird. Ravel told Diamond's violin teacher, André de Ribaupierre, to bring the boy to his hotel the next day. When they arrived, Diamond saw Ravel dressed as brightly as a "walking rainbow": white hair, turquoise tie, purple shirt, orange jacket, dark-green trousers, and golf-style shoes in two shades of brown and white. Diamond recalled the composer's greeting with emotion: "He pulled me in to him, I felt I liked him, he embraced me, gave me a kiss on both cheeks, and kissed me on the neck. From the age of eight I had always known I liked boys, and I was so touched that he kissed me on the neck that I can still feel that kiss."

Ravel advised the boy to study counterpoint with Nadia

Boulanger, saying, "*Il faut que vous* 'study' (pronounced 'stoody')." Ravel asked de Ribaupierre detailed questions about Diamond's family and was intrigued that they were Jewish. He nicknamed Diamond "le Diamant," "Poil de Carotte," or just "Carotte," and the boy, clearly dazzled, wrote to him every week after he returned to France. Diamond recalls, "He had a lovely baritone voice, and fabulous eyes, hazel with a little bit of green. He would take my hand and hold it in his hands."

Later, when the adult Diamond went to study in France, he became friends with André Gide and told the writer that he'd gone to see Ravel. *"Et alors?"* [Well? And . . . ?] Gide asked, alluding to the mystery of Ravel's sexuality. Diamond told Gide, "He gave me a kiss." "Where, when?" exclaimed the fascinated Gide. Diamond added, "I feel in my heart that he likes me a lot." Gide replied, nodding his head, "Not bad, not bad at all."

Ravel's busy schedule did not always permit such gratifying encounters. The *Musical Courrier* treated Ravel's appearance in Kansas City like a hog-weighing contest, estimating that Ravel was "about five feet three inches in height, weight, I should judge, a hundred and fifteen pounds." Other critics described his "figure of a child" and "flyweight" appearance. The *Kansas City Times* said that Ravel looked "interesting rather than handsome, with features a bit too large for so small a head."

Ravel's constant movement was noted. He walked twelve miles a day, he told one interviewer, who added, "He walked fully half that distance during a half-hour interview in the narrow confines of his bedroom. He can't keep still." One day Ravel boarded the train without an interpreter, and frantic hosts sent a telegram to the conductor ordering the composer's lunch: "LAMB CHOPS STRINGBEANS AND COFFEE."

During his American adventure he saw fellow musicians like Bartók and Varèse, and he met George Gershwin, who wanted to take lessons with him. Ravel advised against it, saying that it was better to write good Gershwin than bad Ravel. In Hollywood he met Mary Pickford and Douglas Fairbanks and was relieved that the latter spoke good French. He just missed meeting Charlie Chaplin but rationalized that the two men shared no common language. Even more than artistic meetings, Ravel was enchanted with the phenomenon of the American bathroom and could not wait to remodel his own *salle de bains* in Montfort with American plumbing.

In April 1928 he sent a postcard to the Delages showing "The Old Absinthe House," New Orleans, offering his friends a phonetic spelling of the city's name: "Here is a corner of 'New Olinns.' The streets are called Bourbon, Moyshe, etc. . . . Above all, there are niggers."

At the Rice Institute in Houston, Ravel delivered a speech for which he was paid five hundred dollars, with a further fifteen hundred dollars for performances there. Ravel turned to Roland-Manuel, a fluent journalist, as literary amanuensis, urging him in a letter to "send the lecture" in order that he might collect the fee. The fact that Roland-Manuel, and not Ravel, probably wrote the Rice Institute lecture does not invalidate it. By 1928 Roland-Manuel knew his friend's opinions on musical matters well, even if the tone was too long-winded and stuffy.

Arriving back in France at Le Havre on April 27, Ravel was

met by a small welcoming committee including his brother Edouard, Jourdan-Morhange, Delage, and others. Ravel yelled at his friends from the top of the gangway, "Wait till you see the amazing neckties I've brought!"

Shortly after his return, a friend, the sculptor and interior designer Léon Leyritz, finished a sculpted portrait of Ravel from photographs and invited the composer to come see it. Ravel said he'd stop by Leyritz's studio sometime between 11 P.M. and 3 A.M. and indeed arrived at 1 A.M., with a dozen people in tow. Ravel took one look at the streamlined image, an abstracted version of his face, and screamed, "It's a real photograph!" and inscribed sheet music to Leyritz, "To my dear photographer." The sculpted head is a hard masculine image, with sharp-cut lines, a concentration of Art Deco style and force. A party held in Ravel's garden in Montfort to unveil the new bust, the so-called Impromptu of Montfort, brought together musical friends like Ibert, Honegger, Jourdan-Morhange, the young composer Pierre-Octave Ferroud, and Joaquin Nin, father of the diarist Anaïs Nin. There were also former *Apaches* like Fargue and René Kerdyk, who had been at the Conservatoire with Ravel.

Kerdyk wrote an homage in doggerel to Ravel, which he recited after the company had drunk a good deal. A friend, Pierre Vellones, suggested to Kerdyk that he dress up "as a *tragédienne*," and Kerdyk hastily put on powder, lipstick, rouge, cotton in his cheeks and a dress, to be presented by Vellones to the partygoers as "*Mademoiselle Romunic-Objet* [Miss Rome-Unique Thing] of the Comédie-française." The fifty-year-old poet launched into his mock-epic with sincere affection for Ravel, beginning, "In the absence of Talazac . . ." This was a reference to an obese soprano, Odette Talazac, whose favorite joke was to shout, "Ravel, marry me. . . . We'd make too pretty a couple!" which made Ravel laugh till he cried. At the end of the party, Ravel himself borrowed the hat and coat of two women guests and did a dance in drag.

Afterwards, the local rumor in town was that Ravel's fifty guests had stripped naked during the party and "engaged in curious bacchanalia." Hearing about this imaginative gossip from a friend, Ravel replied, "That's just what my housekeeper heard at the market. Isn't it a disgrace?" Once again Panic and Bacchic reveling pursued Ravel, creating a diabolical image of the artist as orgiastic transgressor.

There was another sign of an odd rapport with Montfort residents when Ravel's beloved Siamese cat, Mouni, was "deliberately poisoned" by a neighbor, according to Jourdan-Morhange. One can only guess at local motivations, but deliberate cruelty to Ravel shocks us, given his apparent kindess to all. Yet the provocative sides of his personality, which he did not often show in public, may have been responsible for such nasty revenge. Ravel's beloved family of Siamese cats all ended unhappily, for the male disappeared and the female "died of grief," even before Mouni met his tragic fate. Ravel never replaced them, wrote Jourdan-Morhange, because he preferred "the certainty of not being hurt to the risks of pleasure."

In contrast to Leyritz's work, another marble portrait of Ravel was made around this time by Louise Ochsé, the wife of Fernand Ochsé, an amateur composer and heir to a chocolate fortune. Ravel enjoyed visiting the Ochsé apartment behind the Panthéon in Paris' fifth arrondissement, filled with automata that served coffee and even played the violin. Years later, the Jewish couple was deported and murdered in Auschwitz. Louise Ochsé's bust of Ravel, reproduced in *La Revue musicale*, showed a fragile, wounded-bird persona, unlike the assertive hardness of Leyritz's work. For public consumption, Ravel clearly preferred the masculine hardness of the Leyritz portrait, but taken together, the two busts provide a yin and yang of Ravel iconography.

Recognitions accumulated: In October 1928 he accepted an honorary doctorate from Oxford University, conferred by a public speaker who aptly remarked in Latin that Ravel was a "charming artist who persuades all cultured people that Pan is not dead, and that even now Mount Helicon is green." Ravel caused a flurry at Oxford by arriving in town wearing a snakeskin tie, with cigarette case and accessories of the same material.

As usual, Ravel stayed in London with his friend Louise Alvar, whose son Charles was playing *Jeux d'eau* on the piano one day when he returned from a concert. Ravel sat down and chimed in with *Tea for Two* while *Jeux d'eau* continued. In 1933 Alvar-Harding observed, "It may seem strange, but the blend was very effective, and Ravel is still faithful today to his affection for [*Tea for Two*]." Shortly after the Oxford doctoral ceremony, Ravel and Charles were standing behind the scenes at a Covent Garden ballet performance, when he overheard people saying in English that a dancer had twisted his ankle and needed a doctor. Fresh from his doctorate at Oxford, Ravel understood only the word *doctor* and turned around, thinking that someone wanted to meet him. He was advancing to greet his supposed visitor when Charles explained the situation. Ravel went up to the dancer and "in the kindest tone, said, 'You have injured yourself dancing to my music and I unfortunately cannot help you, complete 'doctor' though I am.'"

Just before the Oxford visit, Ida Rubinstein, the noted barefoot dancer, commissioned him to orchestrate six pieces from Isaac Albeniz's piano work, *Ibéria*. Joaquin Nin told Ravel that another musician, Enrique Arbos, had the exclusive rights to orchestrate the music and, although Arbos gladly ceded his priority, Ravel decided it would be quicker to write a new piece. This became the fabulously popular *Boléro*.

One morning in 1928, wearing a yellow dressing gown and a scarlet head cap, Ravel played the melody of *Boléro* on the piano for a friend, the critic Gustave Samazeuilh, and asked, "Don't you think this has an insistent quality?"

At first entitled *Fandango,* the ballet was finished in five months. The piece's repetitiveness, and what the composer called its "musico-sexual element" at once made it a popular hit. The relentlessly augmented and varied orchestration culminates in a great climax near the end of the piece, when the tonality is finally modulated, as the key is raised from C major to E major with the effect of a roof blown off a building. This moment of emotion was mocked by Florent Schmitt who, arriving late one day for a concert performance of *Boléro,* explained, "I've just come for the modulation." But a neighbor of Ravel's at Montfort-l'Amaury, a carpenter, often put *Boléro* on his record player, only listening to the first of the two 78 RPM records; when Ravel asked why, the neighbor replied, "There's no point in listening to the other one, it's the same thing!"

At the first performances, Edouard Ravel saw an old lady gripping the back of her seat furiously and shrieking, *"Au fou! Au fou!*

au fou!" [Help the madman! The madman! The madman!] When he heard this story, Ravel said, "That lady . . . she understood!" He joked that *Boléro* was "my masterpiece—too bad there isn't any music in it." But *Boléro* offers many occasions for musicianship, its orchestration showing faith in the capacity of musicians to maintain the continuity of the piece and express emotions within restrictions. *Boléro* immediately reveals the musicianly qualities of an orchestra. With the continuous balance between soloists, and the incessant drum, from the beginning the piece has the energy lift of Elgar's sinuous *March of the Mogul Emperors.* Nothing impedes its monomaniacal progress, with pizzicati as part of a sound texture as complex as any Asian orchestra. A highlight is the trombone part, with saucy slurs and panache, wailing raucously like an elephant seeking a lost spouse. At full orchestral volume, the effect is celebratory and festive, like a Latin street celebration. The final flourish has an orchestral-sized cymbal crash like a guillotine, or, as Manuel Rosenthal said, the ending was "as if someone cut off your head abruptly."

Though Ravel was certain *Boléro* would never be programmed at Sunday concerts because of the sexual element in the work, Robert Casasdesus recalled him saying, "The piece I am working on will be so popular, even fruit peddlers will whistle it in the street." Five years later in Rome, Casadesus was awakened at seven A.M. by a fruit peddler whistling *Boléro* in the street.

In America *Boléro* was used as background music for girlie shows like the Earl Carroll Vanities and was soon recorded on a whole collection of unlikely instruments, from the harmonica to the accordion. Serious musicians were struck by *Boléro,* to the point of obsession. Nathan Milstein complained that the melody was a "depressing tune that gets you everywhere, like a nightmare." In 1930, Sergey Prokofiev was so tormented by an upstairs neighbor in the elegant seventh arrondissement of Paris who incessantly played a gramophone record of *Boléro,* that he declaimed Russian proverbs about the importance of quiet in the home. And when Dmitri Shostakovich wrote his Seventh Symphony in 1941 after fleeing a besieged Leningrad, he told the composer Khachaturian, "Forgive me, will you, if this reminds you of Ravel's *Boléro.*" He told another Soviet composer, Isaak Glikman, "Idle critics will no doubt reproach me for imitating Ravel's *Boléro*; well, let them, for this is how I hear the war." Lennox Berkeley commented that *Boléro* was "a wonderful idea, brilliantly executed, but one feels that such a method of composing is too arbitrary to lead anywhere, and its final paroxysm so calculated that it can only thrill once—however, it is better to be thrilled once than not at all."

In January 1930, Ravel recorded *Boléro* with the Lamoureux orchestra, one of the only versions that maintains a genuinely steady tempo from beginning to end. A few months later, Arturo Toscanini conducted the New York Philharmonic at the Paris Opéra in a controversial interpretation. The soprano Eva Gauthier sat next to Ravel during the concert; she had seen posters announcing the Toscanini performance and was astonished that Ravel was unaware of it and had not been invited. Getting on the phone, she obtained invitations for the composer and herself. But Toscanini had imposed a rigid policy barring latecomers, and because of Ravel's perpetual lateness, they had to wait in the Opéra corridors for the first part of the concert. By the time they were admitted, Ravel snapped that he would leave right after

Boléro, which Gauthier refused to do. First they heard Toscanini conducting Debussy's *La Mer,* and Ravel said, "You know, even though it is not Debussy's best work, it is the one that opened the way for all of us; it needs all the interpretation that Toscanini can give it. But my *Boléro* must not be interpreted."

When *Boléro* began, Ravel was, wrote Gauthier, "fit to be tied" and kept saying loudly, "Three times too fast!" to the annoyance of people sitting nearby. When the piece was over, Toscanini beckoned the composer to rise, but he refused. Everyone urged him, and Gauthier said, "Well, at least get up for France," but Ravel sat stonelike. Gauthier adds, "He was very hurt and felt that he had been slighted in his own country." After sitting out the rest of the concert, he disappeared backstage and "buttonholed Toscanini, whom he really admired, and they had it out for fifteen or twenty minutes." Gauthier was concerned that Toscanini would be offended, but the maestro continued to conduct *Boléro,* the second suite from *Daphnis et Chloé,* and *Pictures at an Exhibition* in his own way, not Ravel's, during the rest of his European tour.

Ravel softened his hard line about Toscanini in a letter to Hélène Casella in May 1930, admitting, "But anyway, he's a marvellous virtuoso, as marvellous as his orchestra." By then the Ravel-Toscanini disagreement had been splashed over the world's media, which made other conductors nervous. If Ravel didn't like Toscanini, what would he say about their own performances, and would it get into the newspapers? Willem Mengelberg stated that he was uneasy about Ravel's presence at a concert where he played *Boléro,* and Clemens Krauss at a Vienna concert was so careful not to play the piece too fast that he took a tempo far too slow, and in the audience Marguerite Long turned to Ravel, triumphantly saying, "You see? It's your own fault!"

Ravel was amused when Paramount Pictures paid him for the "screen rights" to *Boléro,* only to find afterwards that it was not an opera or even a song, and thus had no "story line." A film, *Bolero,* was released in 1934 starring Carole Lombard, George Raft, and Sally Rand doing a fan dance.

After the *Boléro* premiere, a rapid tour of Spain followed—nine cities in eighteen days, including a flop of a recital at Malaga, with Madeleine Grey, where the public left gradually throughout the entire concert until almost no one remained for the curtain call. An amused Ravel told Grey that it was like Haydn's *Farewell Symphony.*

Around 1929 a pair of predatory young men latched onto Ravel, as Jourdan-Morhange recalled: "A certain young man and his comrade . . . followed Ravel around everywhere for six months, going to fetch him in Montfort, taking him to dinner in Paris, following him to nightclubs and to friends' homes." After several months of this, he asked Jourdan-Morhange, "What was the name again of that young man who is always with me?" Soon the young man, who was understood by Ravel's entourage to be gay, organized a series of concerts at Biarritz using Ravel's name but failed to pay the musicians and absconded with the receipts. When the swindle was discovered, Ravel did not prosecute the offending young man but quietly paid the musicians out of his own pocket. Jourdan-Morhange recounted the anecdote as an example of Ravel's absent-mindedness, ignoring its echo of homosexual blackmail.

In 1928 Ravel began thinking about writing a piano concerto. He also planned an opera about Joan of Arc, based on a popular novel by French writer Joseph Delteil and to some extent inspired by the 1925 French production of Bernard Shaw's *Saint Joan* by Georges and Ludmilla Pitoëff. Delteil's novel mixed periods and styles. Although set in the Middle Ages, the novel features characters singing the "Marseillaise" and eating chocolate and brie cheese. Delteil explained that he saw Joan as "a stenographer, or a shopgirl at the Galéries Lafayette." The novelist fully explored Joan's androgynous nature, portraying the popular worship of her as frankly sexual. As Joan rode by on horseback, "young people kissed her thighs with smacking lips." A drawing for Ravel's projected opera by Luc-Albert Moreau shows a sturdy young Joan with a sword standing suggestively between her muscular thighs, both hands on its haft.

Shaw's *Saint Joan,* like Delteil's novel, mixed modern and ancient elements: At the end of the play, a man appears dressed in 1920s garb, and Shaw's tough, ironic humor must have appealed to the composer along with the Russian style of dreamy mysticism in the Pitoëff production. In interviews Ravel described his plans to use musical collages of the "Marseillaise," which suggests a hybrid like Tchaikovsky's *1812 Overture,* although Ravel probably had something subtler in mind, even if his avowed models for the Joan of Arc project were Meyerbeer's operas. Ever open to recuperating the best of composers others considered second-rate, like Saint-Saëns, Ravel appreciated the grand sweep of Meyerbeer's stage works, preferring their orchestrations to Wagner's. Without deluding himself that such "recuperated" composers were on the level of Mozart or Mendelssohn, he nevertheless found that much was to be learned from what they achieved. Conventional piety, however, was not a motivation. His house was located distressingly near a church whose bells rang every morning at six, just as he was getting to sleep, and when a visiting journalist asked if the Joan project was inspired by the carillon, Ravel replied," Your church bells bore the shit out of me."

Shortly after his American tour, Ravel gave a performance at Saint-Jean-de-Luz with the pianist Robert Casadesus to a nearly empty concert hall. The mayor of Saint-Jean-de-Luz was a personal friend. Feeling embarrassed by the local neglect, he planned a Ravel festival for 1930, during which Ciboure renamed the street where the composer was born Quai Maurice Ravel, an honor usually reserved for the dead. A pelota match was held, featuring stars of the sport who came specially to honor this son of the Basque country, and Ravel was touched by the gesture. When the time came for the official mayoral procession to Ravel's birthplace, the composer turned "crimson with embarrassment" and begged Robert and Gaby Casadesus to sneak off with him and drink a cherry brandy: "I don't want to be so ridiculous as to attend the dedication of my own plaque." The three escaped to a local café where they sat outside, safely hidden by a hedge of small trees, listening to the "town band bravely playing in the distance for the great composer who did not appear." Casadesus later recalled that Ravel did attend a concert of his works that evening, where the public "was enormously moved, and Ravel was like a child, amazed at the emotion his music had evoked."

Meanwhile, the composer was going ahead with sketches for a piano concerto in G Major, when out of the blue he received a commission from the Austrian pianist Paul Wittgenstein, who had lost an arm in the war, for a concerto for the left hand only. Wittgenstein, the brother of the philosopher Ludwig Wittgenstein, commissioned a number of other composers for left-handed works, among them Richard Strauss, Hindemith, Prokofiev, and Britten. An ornery and autocratic person with a short military haircut like Erich von Stroheim, Wittgenstein was by nature a disapproving sort. He wrote to Sergey Prokofiev on receiving that composer's Fourth Concerto, for the Left Hand, "Thank you for your concerto, but I do not understand a single note and I shall not play it."

Paul Wittgenstein's playing was not admired by his own family, who thought he "lacked taste" and was "too full of extravagant gestures," but Wittgenstein himself felt it was "important to be respected and even feared." Soon after he lost his arm, he took boxing lessons to learn how to fight with the remaining one. The "harsh and secretive strain in his personality" became clearer when he left his wife years later and turned out to have been leading a double life in a love nest with another woman.

To prepare for the technical challenges of writing the *Concerto pour la main gauche seule* [Concerto for the Left Hand Alone] as he called it at first, Ravel studied exercises for the left hand by Czerny, Alkan, and Weber, but found that only Saint-Saëns's *Six études pour la main gauche* was useful. Ravel wrote the work with passion. In the draft copy of the score, he crossed out a blank page between pages 45 and 46 with pen strokes of uncanny violence and intensity, expressing furnace-heat emotion. The title as cited in early letters and manuscripts is *Concerto pour la main gauche seule*, later abbreviated to *Concerto pour la main gauche*, but the word *seule*, evocative of solitude and dismemberment, might be retained as the composer first intended.

The concerto is distinguished throughout by its anguished tone and mix of musical styles, from what sounds like a traditional classical concerto to more jazzy variants. The concerto is in one movement, lasting about twenty minutes. Tragedy and torment are keynotes of the work. Low somber foghorn notes at the beginning suggest an ominous sea voyage, like the beginning of *La Valse.* They set the scene for the tragic message to come. Ravel clearly intended, as with *La Valse,* to express a Germanic cultural background for the concerto, into which a big hand introduces itself with impressive configurations for the piano. Jacques Février, a friend of Ravel's from his own childhood who toured with the concerto all over the world, was able to stretch his hand to encompass the digital extension required. Small-handed pianists found the work literally out of their reach. Devilish technical difficulty, along with the malicious tone of somber moments, show that, as in *Scarbo,* the devil may again have been at work. Taking a page from Schumann's song setting of Heine's *Old Evil Songs* in *Dichterliebe,* Ravel created some new evil music to match the ominous time it was written in, shortly before World War II.

Beginning with a slowly rocking rhythm, the concerto speeds up until the orchestra unites with the tympani against the soloist. Suddenly the piece breaks into a ribald war march, like an episode out of Stravinsky's *Soldier's Tale.* At times the orchestra seems to make sarcastic comments about the pianist's difficulties. In the central section, there is Spanish music of triumph, like the fanfare at the end of a *corrida*—and a bullfight it certainly is for the soloist. When Casadesus performed the concerto in Mexico, the conductor Carlos Chavez (himself a composer) gave as an encore an orchestral piece usually played to honor the toreador after the kill, much to the pianist's amusement.

Alfred Cortot, a great musician but uneven technician, insisted on playing the "*Concerto pour la main gauche*" using both hands. What seemed normal to Cortot was a bad joke and musical betrayal for Ravel, who publicly opposed such performances, insisting that the piece was conceived and written for one hand only. So Cortot waited till Ravel died, and then, in 1939, recorded the "*Concerto pour la main gauche*" still using two hands.

At a party in Vienna, where Wittgenstein played an informal premiere of the *Concerto pour la main gauche,* he told Marguerite Long that he had made a few "arrangements" in the work. She thought these might have been due to his war injury, which was not actually the case, and advised him to warn Ravel beforehand, which Wittgenstein declined to do. During the performance, Ravel's face "darkened more and more." As soon as it was over, Long tried to "stage a diversion" by chatting loudly and energetically with Vienna's French ambassador, but Ravel moved slowly over to Wittgenstein and said, "That's not it at all." Wittgenstein, ever stubborn, said, "I'm an old pianist and it doesn't sound right," to which Ravel replied, "I'm an old orchestrator and it sounds right!"

Ravel was so furious that he cancelled the car waiting for himself and Long, and both walked back to their hotel in bitter cold. Wittgenstein followed up this scene with a furious letter, saying,

"Interpreters must not be slaves!" To which Ravel replied, "Interpreters *are* slaves!" Wittgenstein believed that the piece sounded better in his version, explaining that when Ravel played it for him, he was less than impressed: "[Ravel] was not an outstanding pianist, and I wasn't overwhelmed by the composition. It always takes me a while to grow into a difficult work. I suppose Ravel was disappointed, and I was sorry, but I had never learned to pretend." Wittgenstein had in fact tinkered with two pages in the middle of the concerto, where he wanted to play the main theme instead of letting the orchestra do it. Ravel thought this "ruined the concerto," and Wittgenstein later had to admit that the composer was right. He did, however, play the concerto in Paris in 1933, and in Monte Carlo, Boston, and New York. After his period of exclusivity was over, Marguerite Long admitted the piece was beyond her and passed it along to her student Jacques Février.

With one piano concerto finished, at the cost of nearly a year of insomnia, Ravel wanted to get back to another one straight away, but exhaustion temporarily intervened. He jokingly referred to the Concerto in G as his Concerto Not for the Right Hand Only, and planned to use it as a vehicle to tour the world, saying that it was "in the same spirit as Mozart and Saint-Saëns." However, his health was bad and he agreed to allow Marguerite Long, a domineering woman and an imperfect pianist, to take the soloist's role. He needed the money from concerts and would often say, "I'm always short 50,000 francs." Manuel Rosenthal later recalled, "With Marguerite Long it was mostly slavery—Ravel being the slave. She paid him for the Concerto in G, true, but that's because she didn't have much outstanding in her repertoire, so he let himself be used. . . . In Marguerite Long's company, [Ravel] spoke like a little boy who had a governess imposed on him. She was a woman to be feared, from every point of view." When Ravel's aphasia later made him forget names but left his musical judgment intact, he referred to Long as "You know, that woman who doesn't play the piano very well." The approximative playing on her recordings of the Concerto in G, including one supervised by Ravel himself, have long mystified listeners, but the composer's attitude toward her playing was like his attitude at his own concerts, accepting performance limitations and getting on with the job. With women friends like Long or Jourdan-Morhange, Ravel was gallant and accommodating about technical problems, as if expecting less than he did from male musicians.

First performed on January 14, 1932, at the Salle Pleyel, the Concerto in G is in three movements, *Allegramente, Adagio Assai,* and *Presto.* Ravel's comment that interpreters "are slaves" may have something to do with the whip crack that begins the Concerto in G, a slave driver's command to get the soloist moving. In ancient Greek myth, Pan's whip made a sound heard by Corybants and other possessed people, who were unable to hear anything else during Panic revelry. The first movement alternates concentrated up-tempo dancing, which has been likened to Basque folk dances, and a languid fantasia—a romantically strummed depiction of a night in a Spanish garden amid passionate high-stepping. The impression is of a ballet with ideas, or a literary-romantic fantasy, like Strauss's *Don Quixote.* Indolent sensuality and brisk virtuosity are akin to those in Saint-Saëns's piano concertos. The second movement is emotive and romantic, with the sad, naked innocence of a Satie waltz. An orchestral palette with the emotional density of Elgar is juxtaposed with a piano sounding, atypically for Ravel, like Bach. In the final movement, with a drumroll, we are back in the circus with mocking wind instruments. At times the horn section seems about to burst into the "Marseillaise," as if referring back to the aborted Joan of Arc opera.

By 1930 Ravel had reached a new plateau of fame and was honored in an essay by Theodor Adorno in the Viennese modern music monthly *Anbruch*. Adorno felt that Ravel, more than Richard Strauss or Busoni, was "the real master of sound-masks." From Adorno's Marxist perspective, the Frenchman belonged to the "aristocratic haute-bourgeoisie," a judgment probably based more on press photos of Ravel in formal garb than on anything in his music.

Adorno called his achievement "wunderkind" music, referring to the composer's "aristocratic sublimation of mourning," and Manuel Rosenthal also felt that in works like *La Valse,* the *Concerto pour la main gauche* and *Boléro,* Ravel expressed the fear of death. He recalled that the composer did not like to walk in the Rambouillet forest near his home in autumn, finding it too funereal. Ravel would say, "It's death, all those leaves on the ground, they're going to rot."

Concerned by Ravel's night-long rambles, heavy smoking, and other excesses, his brother, Edouard, and surrogate parents, the Bonnets, asked Léon Leyritz to design a special room for the composer in their podgy house on an industrial street in the Paris suburb of Levallois-Perret. Leyritz created an Art Deco dream, with wood paneling and a bar that emerged from the foot of a bed; this was in homage to Ravel's craze for inventing cocktails, to which he gave names like Phi-Phi (the title of a French *operette*). Leyritz shut off the ugly street view with bottle-lens distorting glass embedded in the windows. Despite these efforts, Ravel spent almost no time in the room, preferring his more independent disarray at Monfort-l'Amaury and the liberating travel of concert tours.

Casting about for new projects, Ravel considered two new commissions: a ballet for Ida Rubinstein, *Morgiane,* based on the story of Ali Baba and the Forty Thieves from the *1001 Nights* and songs for a film of Don Quixote, with Chaliapin in the title role. The film's director was G. W. Pabst, famous for his film version of the *Threepenny Opera* of 1931.

Unbeknown to Ravel, a number of composers, including Jacques Ibert, Milhaud, and Delannoy, were also commissioned to write music for the film. Ibert's songs were finally used, provoking talk of a lawsuit from Ravel, which apparently petered out. Ravel chose as texts three poems by a friend, the novelist, diplomat, and high-society playboy Paul Morand, whose poetic output was sparse. Morand's "pretentious" Don Quixote lyrics, as Vladimir Jankélévitch called them, remained unpublished outside of Ravel's musical score. The first lyric, *Don Quichotte à Dulcinée* is particularly awkward, with the word "offensa" [offended] rhyming with "Sancho Panza." The simple directness of the songs may have been intended to counteract the hamming of Chaliapin, who could chew scenery relentlessly. Already in 1913, Ravel had complained about Chaliapin's Boris: "There is no need to add these sinister sniggers, these cavernous sighs that have such a gross and unmusical effect." It was probably just as well he didn't know about Chaliapin's onstage habit of screaming anti-Semitic insults at a conductor when he lost his own way vocally during performances. The second song, *Chanson épique*, exploited Chaliapin's admirable vocal high range. The "amen" at the end of the song, also at the upper end of the voice, is reminiscent of Desdemona's "amen" at the end of the *Ave Maria* aria in Verdi's *Otello*. The third song, *Chanson à boire*, also recalls *Otello*, echoing the baritone coloratura of Iago's drinking aria in the first act.

Not long after finishing these songs, while riding in a taxi in October 1932, Ravel was involved in a collision which left him with facial cuts and a bruised chest and thorax. Although shaken up, he was not at first considered to be seriously harmed, but grave consequences soon became apparent. He probably did not realize then that the *Don Quichotte* melodies would prove to be his swan song as a composer.

CHAPTER 7

Decline and Apotheosis

1933–1937

As the 1930s wore on, Ravel was not only obsessed with his own health but kept an eye open on world events, receiving visits from refugees who were fleeing Fascist Europe. He wrote generous checks for these sufferers, although his own income remained moderate. In January 1933 Guido Gatti, director of the Florence Festival, fired the Jewish singer Madeleine Grey, who was scheduled to perform *Chansons madécasses,* because of Mussolini's anti-Semitic laws. Ravel's letter of protest had no effect, and the composer apologized to Grey for not having taken into account "the laws of Fascism." Had he remained in good health, there is little doubt that Ravel would have been a stout-hearted opponent of the Fascist monstrosities to come.

On January 17, 1933, the *Concerto pour la main gauche* had its Paris premiere, with Paul Wittgenstein playing under the direction of the composer. (The world premiere in Vienna, over a year before, had been conducted by Robert Heger, mostly known as an operetta composer and conductor.) Soon after the Paris concert, Wittgenstein and Ravel were supposed to repeat the performance in Monte Carlo, but Ravel, feeling poorly, was replaced by Paul Paray. In the summer of 1933 Ravel's health worsened dramatically. He usually swam with ease and pleasure, but one day at the beach he forgot the basic movements. Trying to skim a pebble across the water, his hand lashed out of control and threw it at the head of a woman he was with (probably Jourdan-Morhange).

He felt better in November and conducted an orchestral program in Paris, but soon he was at a loss for familiar words and names. Unable to recall the name of Darius Milhaud, he would say, "You know the one I mean. . . . His health is bad. . . . His wife drives the car." To refer to his housekeeper, Madame Révelot, he would say, "You know, the lady who takes care of the house, who has a nasty personality." As his illness developed, he could only play successive octaves on a piano if someone lifted his hands off one octave and placed them on the next. He forgot common words and needed a dictionary to write a letter, and a photo from this time, inscribed to "Margueritte" Long, calls her the "record-holdder" of his concerto.

The three *Don Quichotte* songs were first performed at a concert of the Colonne orchestra, sung by baritone Martial Singher and conducted by Paul Paray. Singher was a refined artist who especially pleased Ravel because he was of Basque origin, born in Biarritz.

Cinema provided a temporary diversion; at a 1933 outing Ravel was fascinated by James Whale's *The Invisible Man,* starring Claude Rains. He was obsessed by the last scene, when the Invisible Man becomes visible bit by bit after death. Manuel Rosenthal recalled, "This sight put Ravel in a trance—how many times he spoke to me about it. Of course, in itself, it's magic, but I wonder if in his mind it didn't have some rapport with musical composition . . . the death of the Invisible Man being at the same time the resurrection of the artist." If artistic resurrection had been the reason for Ravel's emotion, surely he would not have reacted with such sadness; yet he "always choked up when he spoke of it, with great emotion, almost a sob."

Ravel had occasionally been impressed by the cinema. The portrait of insanity in *The Cabinet of Doctor Caligari,* Chaplin's tragicomic grace, and Fritz Lang's mechanical vision of man's future in *Metropolis* could inspire him. But his response to *The Invisible Man* was unique in its intensity and duration. Ravel's private life was usually invisible even to his close friends, but after death, all might become visible. He could not have known that the British director of *The Invisible Man,* James Whale, whose Hollywood career was ruined because he refused to conceal his homosexuality, is believed to have given a gay subtext to his film.

Ravel was also an Invisible Man in his recordings, where he was often replaced by more skillful musicians. This created some confusion in attributions. Performances listing Ravel as pianist were in fact sometimes played by Robert Casadesus, at the composer's request, and pieces that were really led by the Portuguese conductor Pedro Freitas-Branco were marketed as being conducted by Ravel himself, as we have seen.

Despite what he thought was cerebral anemia, Ravel continued to make projects. The British violist Lionel Tertis visited him in the early thirties and commissioned a work. Ravel was "charming and complimentary" and said he'd write something for viola, small orchestra, and concealed humming chorus (*bouches fermées*). Tertis recalled that there would be an alternative part for harmonium, if a choir were unavailable. Ravel's rapid decline prevented the project from being realized.

Anguish about his condition led to atypical outbursts in public, such as the one at a Paris concert by the Brazilian pianist Magda Tagliaferro, where Manuel Rosenthal's *Petit Metiers* was played. Reynaldo Hahn was sitting on Rosenthal's left and Ravel on his right, and Hahn started to chat with a lady while Rosenthal's work was being performed. Ravel furiously yelled at Hahn that he was "not fit to listen to this music" and other insults, in a scene that recalls Fokine's moralistic denunciation of Diaghilev.

As his health declined, Ravel's fame was at its height, and frustrated journalists were avid for interviews that he could no longer give. In September 1933 the American music writer David Ewen, starting his career as a prolific author, apparently forged an interview with Ravel for *The Etude,* according to Arbie Orenstein. When protests came from the Ravel entourage that the interview could not have taken place, Ewen was admonished and fired from the magazine, but three years later he published a clear forgery in the January 1936 issue of *B'nai Brith Magazine,* "Maurice Ravel on Jewish Music."

Ravel was still able to offer advice to students and young composers, like the twenty-one-year-old David Diamond, who visited Montfort with his composition *Psalm*. When Diamond explained that the work was inspired by Oscar Wilde's tomb at Père Lachaise, Ravel stared at him, saying, *"Sans blague . . . invraisemblable . . .*

ça alors." [No kidding ... unbelievable ... what next!] Diamond's work was dedicated to his friend Gide, and Ravel wanted to know how often he saw Gide, if Gide liked Diamond and who Gide was seeing these days. The violinist Maurice Hewitt, who was bisexual, later told Diamond that Ravel appreciated the younger man's "allure." Hewitt added, "You must have fascinated Ravel a great deal, as a person," said Hewitt. Diamond reflected about his own relationship with Ravel: "We might have become great friends, if he had lived. Ravel was very amused when I went into the bathroom next to his bedroom and commented on his huge, deep bathtub, which he said was for sleepless nights, when he would get in and float." Diamond added wistfully, "I wish I could have seen him taking a bath!" During one 1936 visit, Diamond told Ravel how he enjoyed visiting the brothel Le Sphinx to chat with the old prostitutes, whose tales reminded him of his mother. Ravel exclaimed with shocked amusement, *"Ta mère!? Ça alors! C'est moche, ça!"* [Your mother? What next! Ooh, that's nasty!].

His condition continued to decline, and his thoughts went to his father's last years, when he was exhausted and depressed. A cure at a Swiss clinic, Mon Repos on Mont Pélérin, did little to help; as he reported to Lucien Garban, "It's cerebral anemia in all its horror." In January 1935 he wrote a public statement intended to help his bizarre student Obouhov. The next month he was present at a concert of the Pasdeloup orchestra, conducted by Piero Coppola, which included the first performance of an orchestrated version of his song *Ronsard à son âme,* which he had dictated to Manuel Rosenthal and Lucien Garban, since he could no longer write music manually.

Ida Rubinstein, observing Ravel's health problems with increasing concern, sent him on holiday to Spain and Morocco, ostensibly to gather atmosphere for the ballet *Morgiane,* which she had commissioned. In the *1001 Nights,* Morgiane (Marjana) rescues Ali Baba and arranges for the death of the forty thieves, which would have been a masculine, assertive role for the manly Rubinstein. Ravel told Hélène Jourdan-Morhange about his plans for *Morgiane:* "It'll be magnificent. There'll be blood, voluptuousness and death. And I'll do it like Massenet." Friends hoped that Ravel, chaperoned by the loyal Leyritz, would be distracted from his health torments. Rubinstein was in contact by phone each day with the travelers, suggesting new delights to entertain Ravel.

When Leyritz and Ravel arrived in Marrakesh, they stayed at the luxurious Hotel Mamounia, where Ravel leaned over the balcony, as was his wont, and "marvelled at the water carriers, magnificent-looking young Moroccan men whose light-blue short pants revealed lovely muscled bronze legs," as Jourdan-Morhange later wrote. Ravel compared them to biblical characters, only to be rudely awakened to reality when one of them began to whistle *Boléro.* The composer stared with fascination at the dyers' souk, where men with nude torsos, purple hands, and red or yellow arms leaned forward over vats of dye.

During their stay in Marrakesh, Leyritz and Ravel spent an evening with Si Mammeri, "the local music lover," who showed them Chleuh (Berber) dances, rituals "in which women's roles are danced by frail boys, whose ambiguous beauty is very close—too close—to feminine grace. These dances suggest sacrificial rites, and Ravel, that night representing 'God,' was a bit disturbed to see these young servants coming to place imaginary garlands at his feet, or the symbols that his amused mind could suggest to him," Jourdan-Morhange reported.

Ravel communed with nature and local young men. Walking one night with an Arab lad, Ravel marveled at his good French, whereupon "little Omar" replied lazily, "Oh, I worked as a waiter for two years in Paris at the Duchesse de Clermont-Tonnerre's." When Ravel praised the beauty of the sky, the blasé Omar said, "That's nothing today; some nights, the sky opens, only not everyone can see it." As Omar may still be alive as an octogenarian circa 2000, more details of this trip could be forthcoming. Ida Rubinstein was eager to try anything to stimulate the maestro's creativity, and the program of wish-fulfillment fantasies included snake charmers. Leyritz reported that Ravel, "as a spoiled grown-up child, found it natural to live in the supernatural climate of fairy tales." Ravel always enjoyed quoting Oscar Wilde's maxim "Nature imitates art," so whether the shows were staged or not meant little.

Musically, Ravel was not overwhelmed by what he heard on his trip, saying, "If I were to write something Arab, it would be more Arab than all this." He also complained about the food, grilled chicken eaten with one's fingers and vegetables cooked "in four-year-old rancid butter." But at a house in Fez there was a pleasurable reception with more cats than people. Ravel called it the "cat soirée," and a dozen felines climbed on him to be petted, whereupon he said, "You see, they know I'm the one who's their lover." There were some dark moments too, as a friend, Jean-Louis Lévi-Alvarès, recounted: After a sumptuous banquet, a French army officer suggested that they all go out to the desert and try some "target practice on the natives." Ravel silently got up from the table and walked away quickly, indignant and revolted by the joke.

On his way home through Spain, Ravel made a special trip to the church of San Antonio de la Florida on the outskirts of Madrid, to see the frescoes by Goya from the life of Saint Anthony of Padua. In a scene of the saint bringing a dead man back to life, Goya mixed the historical past and present, as Ravel planned to do in his opera *Joan of Arc.* The 1798 fresco shows a crowd of eighteenth-century Spanish people witnessing the saint's miracle, with excited children impishly climbing over a railing with the same magical devilishness that Ravel found in child-hood. And he shared with Goya a taste for human monsters. As Baudelaire wrote in 1857 in "Some Foreign Caricaturists," Goya created a "credible form of the monstrous. His monsters are born viable, harmonious. . . . All those distortions, those bestial faces, those diabolic grimaces of his are impregnated with humanity." The same is true of Ravel.

During this brief interlude, Ravel made some notes for *Morgiane,* and wrote a letter to his brother, Edouard, but his illness continued its course. A letter was written for him in May 1937, to protest his inclusion in a *Dictionary of Jews in Music,* pub-lished by a Nazi musicologist in Munich, Hans Brückner. In a stiff style, the letter seems to have been written for Ravel by his lawyer or publisher, pointing out that Ravel was not Jewish and demanding that his name be taken out of each copy of the book and a correction be printed in German newspapers. The musicol-ogist replied with a letter reeking of Bavarian charm, agreeing to remove Ravel's name from future editions of the book and signing himself "your completely devoted Brückner." The last known letter written and signed by Ravel was to the conductor Ernst Ansermet in October 1937, advising him against hiring Alfred Cortot for a performance of his *Concerto pour la main gauche,* because Cortot still insisted on using both hands to play the work.

Ravel much preferred working with Jacques Février, who performed the concerto often and recorded it three times. Février was the only person, besides his family and two or three old schoolfriends like Ricardo Viñes, with whom Ravel used the informal *tu* form of address. This was because he had known Février from the cradle (he was born in 1900); according to friends, as Ravel's confidant, Février knew more than anyone else about the composer's sexual interest in young men.

In June 1937 he managed to offer advice to Madeleine Grey, who was planning to sing *Don Quichotte à Dulcinée* at a concert accompanied by Francis Poulenc. Not disapproving of this transposition of sexes, Ravel only objected when the performers added a rubato during rehearsal which was not in the written score, and he pointed to the relevant section of music. Given Ravel's incapacity to speak and his weakness, Grey and Poulenc were amazed that he was able to discern such a fine musical point. Soon after, Ravel attended a concert performance of *Daphnis et Chloé,* conducted by Inghelbrecht, and wept in a taxi afterwards to Jourdan-Morhange, "I haven't said anything, I still have so much to say."

Ravel consulted a number of doctors, especially Pasteur Valléry-Radot, who had been a close friend of Debussy. The medical diagnosis for Ravel's illness was Wernicke's aphasia, which explained his difficulty in speaking, complicated by ataxia, the difficulty in making certain muscular motions. These symptoms, however, did not reveal the underlying cause of the problem.

He was also examined by the eminent neurologist Clovis Vincent, who founded the first neurological clinic at Paris's Hôpital de la Pitié. Decisions about the composer's treatment were made by a committee of male friends and students: Manuel Rosenthal, Roland-Manuel, Maurice Delage, and Ravel's brother, Edouard. Tact was needed to keep the shy, sensitive Edouard from bursting into tears over his brother's condition. Vincent explained the problem in layman's terms, in a voice that had "something child-like about it," according to one colleague. Ravel's brain showed wear and tear after long abuse of his health, including too much smoking, drinking, and staying up all night. His stressful war service aged him prematurely too, no doubt. As a result, one of the brain's lobes had sunk or shrunken a little. Vincent was sure that no tumor was present, and usually he would have argued against surgery, instead letting the afflicted patient go home to decline in a walled-in torture, aware of his own decay. Because the patient was Ravel, Vincent said that even if there was only a tiny percentage of hope, surgery would be worth a try.

Ravel's head was duly shaved and a turban bandage put on, which friends joked made him look like Lawrence of Arabia. The composer replied that he thought he looked like a Moor. Ravel was told only that further X rays were needed, but he sensed that an operation was imminent, telling Rosenthal, "I know that they're going to cut my nut off." (*me couper cabèche*). At the last moment the operation was delayed because a twelve-year-old boy arrived at the hospital emergency ward needing immediate brain surgery, and Vincent decided that the composer could wait. So Ravel had a brief respite, going home overnight where he was surrounded by friends. Listening to the radio, he made a gesture describing a large-chested woman in reference to a fat singer who was performing. He had recognized her voice.

The next day he was operated on. Stravinsky, a ghoulish amateur of surgery wards and deathbeds, who had been absent from Ravel's life for several years, made a sudden reappearance. The Russian stated years later that Ravel "felt the incision." Clovis Vincent surely knew how to anesthetize a patient, and in the early days of neurosurgery, it is unlikely that any of Ravel's pupils or friends would have been permitted to watch the surgery. Someone may have seen a reflex movement by the patient and interpreted it as physical suffering, although it is unclear how Stravinsky might have learned this.

Ravel seemed to recover from the surgery, waking and asking to see his brother, Edouard, but he later sank into unconsciousness and died nine days after the operation, on December 28, 1937. Awkward deathbed drawings by Luc-Albert Moreau show him as a tiny figure with head bandage and gloves like a Disney character. Stravinsky, who made a posthumous visit, said his "arms looked as long as his body." Two days later there was a modest burial service at the Levallois-Perret cemetery, attended by the composer's brother, his only direct survivor, and musical friends like Robert and Gaby Casadesus, Darius and Madeleine Milhaud, Poulenc, and Stravinsky.

Speaking the official eulogy at the cemetery as a representative of the French government, the socialist Minister for Education Jean Zay, a colleague of Léon Blum's in the Front Populaire, compared the dead composer to Schumann, Gérard de Nerval, and other geniuses whose minds became "clouded." The comparison was ill-founded because to the last Ravel remained musically alert and certainly not insane, despite difficulties in expressing himself. Zay, who would soon be murdered by the Milice during the German occupation, was closer to the mark when he said that Ravel belonged to a line of French geniuses including Descartes, Le Nôtre, Racine, Voltaire, Marivaux, Stendhal, Fouquet, Watteau, Ingres, and Cézanne, all of whom shared a lucid, sharplined intelligence.

The day after the composer's death, David Diamond began writing an *Elegy in Memory of Maurice Ravel,* which turned into a sort of pavane for a dead prince, with an insistently driving brass theme that evokes tough solitude and his beloved friend's passion for walking. Ravel's home at Montfort-l'Amaury was preserved by his brother and later opened as a museum. By contrast, the apartment designed for him in Levallois-Perret by Leyritz was dismantled, with the intention that one day it should be displayed at a planned museum of the City of Paris. Somehow the décor was "lost," it is uncertain when. Perhaps today someone in France or abroad is unwittingly living in a home surrounded by Art Deco ornaments designed for the composer.

On May 4, 1966, the *New York Times* headlined a story, "Widower of a Friend Given Ravel's Riches." The article noted: "A former hairdresser, who never had any connection with Maurice Ravel, was ruled today the rightful heir to the composer's royalties, estimated at $200,000 per year" (equivalent now to over two million dollars per year). It reported that a court in Bayonne had dismissed a lawsuit by two distant relatives of the composer, who wanted to invalidate the last will and testament of Edouard Ravel, claiming he was not in his right mind when he signed it. Edouard had left his estate perfectly legally to his masseuse and housekeeper, Mrs. Jeanne Taverne, who had died while the suit was pending. She in turn left her fortune to her husband Alexandre, a hairdresser.

In 1966 an American musicologist, Arbie Orenstein, preparing a Ph.D. thesis on Ravel's vocal music at Columbia University, went to Saint-Jean-de-Luz to ask Alexandre Taverne if there were any unaccounted-for manuscripts. Amid the thousand-odd manuscript pages he uncovered were six previously unknown compositions by Ravel, and they were given world premieres at a Ravel centenary concert held at Queens College on February 23, 1975. They included the *Sonate pour violin et piano* of 1897, the *Sérénade grotesque* of 1893, and four songs from 1893 to 1910. In 1992 the original score of *Boléro* sold at auction in Paris for 1.8 million francs, and the buyer immediately donated it to the Bibliothèque Nationale in order to prevent another important Ravel score from ending up abroad. Unfortunately, the present owner of many important manuscript scores, Madame Alexandre Taverne, the hairdresser's surviving second wife, has not permitted scholars to examine them, which makes serious editions of many Ravel works impossible.

Whatever the destiny of his manuscripts, Ravel's death was sincerely and acutely mourned. Alma Mahler noted in 1937: "Ravel has become a standard *Meister* . . . though I think Debussy and Stravinsky were and are stronger and more original. Ravel is like the moon between two suns." Some friends felt bereft, like Colette, who wrote in a theater review in March 1938 that, after hearing the *Concerto pour la main gauche* played by Jacques Février, she felt "dissatisfied with the poor, weak, and yet sensitive go-between of human speech." Among obituarists, the philosopher and music critic Gabriel Marcel found in Ravel's music "an incapacity to love or to give of oneself, which is self-conscious, and self-pitying." Yet he likened Ravel's "witchery" to the "marvellous magician's technique" of Paul Valéry.

In 1939 the philosopher Vladimir Jankélévitch published a study of Ravel unusual in its density of argument and grasp of the composer's cultural resonance. After the faithful studies by Roland-Manuel, Jankélévitch's book, coming on the eve of World War II and France's disgrace, was a fervent cry of what it meant to be French. On June 11, 1940, just before the French defeat, André Gide noted in his journal that the Pétainist trend was toward denying a "certain mental grace . . . turning our backs on all that French art has produced of delicacy, nuance, and subtlety." He wondered if people would soon be ordered to prefer crass folksongs to Debussy and Ravel.

Among musicians abroad, Ravel's reputation remained high. In 1923 the young music director of the Munich Opera, Karl Böhm, had conducted a double bill of Ravel's *L'Heure espagnole,* with Stravinsky's *Rossignol,* but rehearsals were interrupted by Hitler's march on the Feldherrnhalle, which started a riot. And Otto Klemperer's progressive Kroll Opera in Berlin had staged *L'Heure espagnole* in 1929, skillfully conducted by Alexander von Zemlinsky, with Jarmila Novotna as Concepcion. But musical opinions in France were divided. The influential Olivier Messiaen let his students at the Conservatoire know that he didn't like Ravel's music: "It goes up, up and you think it's going to explode, and then it stops," he said, and tartly observed that in the Concerto in G, Ravel "Massenetized a phrase from Fauré on a bad day." Messiaen's student Pierre Boulez, at his influential "Domaine musicale" concerts in the 1950s, programmed only one work by Ravel, the atypical *Frontispice*. Since then Boulez has conducted uneven recordings of some of Ravel's orchestral music, but real disciples like Marcelle Meyer, Jacques Février, Pedro de Freitas-Branco, Manuel Rosenthal, and others have fortunately made records filled with insights that are of real documentary importance.

Ravel's influence, which had always been wide, has become universal. In 1925 the Polish composer Karol Szymanowski praised Ravel as belonging to the "aristocratic" line of great French composers, and in 1972 a follower of Szymanowski, Witold Lutoslawski, told an audience in Paris that Ravel had influenced his work since at age twelve he first read through *Jeux d'eau* at the piano. He realized for the first time, he said, "the harmonic riches hidden within the twelves tones of the tempered scale. I see Ravel as a classic, a Mozart of our century. And as such, he must be the source of inspiration for all those who want to write durable music, super-temporal, capable of surviving."

Further Reading

Anyone wanting to find out more about Ravel would do well to begin with Arbie Orenstein's *Ravel Reader* (Columbia University Press) and *Ravel: Man and Musician* (Dover). Roger Nichols's study in the Master Musicians series was published in 1977; although now hard to find, it retains its value, as does his more recent *Ravel Remembered* (Faber & Faber). Older studies by Norman Demuth for Dent and Rollo Myers for Duckworth are also worth looking up. Gerald Larner's survey, published by Phaidon in 1997, is disappointingly unoriginal and not free of errors. The best overall study of Ravel's cultural milieu and impact remains Vladimir Jankélévitch's book, originally published by Seuil, and translated into English, as was the study by Ravel's student, Roland-Manuel, published in English by Dobson in 1947. Readers of French might begin with Flammarion's edition of Arbie Orenstein's anthology, *Maurice Ravel: Lettres, Ecrits, Entretiens,* which has the virtue of presenting the documents in their original language.

Further Listening on CD

Among the summits of an unusually rich discography are Pierre Monteux's *Boléro, Ma Mère l'Oye,* and *La Valse* on Philips, and the same conductor's complete *Daphnis et Chloé, Rapsodie espagnole,* and *Pavane pour une infante défunte* on Decca, and his *Shéhérazade* on Music and Arts. All are highly recommended. The second suite from *Daphnis et Chloé* is available conducted by Guido Cantelli on Testament, and on BMG by Arturo Toscanini, who also recorded the Ravel orchestration of Mussorsky's *Pictures at an Exhibition.* It is worth hearing all of Marcelle Meyer's recordings of the piano works as reissued by EMI France. Jascha Heifetz's 1934 recording on BMG of *Tzigane,* accompanied by Arpad Sandor, is an astonishment, and Walter Gieseking's 1929 *Gaspard de la nuit* has been reprinted by Pearl, along with the German pianist's *Alborada del gracioso.* Dinu Lipatti's own *Alborada,* on EMI, is also magical. Other definitive piano performances by Robert Casadesus and Jacques

Février have appeared from EMI France. A complete set of Ravel's mélodies on EMI boasts fine performances by Gabriel Bacquier, José van Dam, and Felicity Lott. The brilliant young violinist Christian Tetzlaff recorded the violin sonata for Virgin, accompanied by the gifted Leif Ove Andsnes. Ernest Ansermet's version of *L'Enfant et les sortilèges* is precious for the presence of the tenor Hugues Cuénod. Singers known and admired by the composer, like Madeleine Grey, Jane Bathori, and Martial Singher, have recorded his works, and their versions have appeared on CD, usually on fugitive labels, but they are worth tracking down. The same is true of the Calvet Quartet's versions of the *Introduction and Allegro,* with flutist Marcel Moyse, and the same group's version of Ravel's Quartet. Overdue for reprinting on CD are Pedro de Freitas-Branco's readings of the orchestral works, originally published by London Records. Also urgently needed on CD are the performances by conductors Gabriel Pierné, Walther Straram, and Philippe Gaubert, as no one today conducts Ravel with the depth of understanding of these three old masters.

Bibliography

Ackere, Jules van. *Maurice Ravel*. Brussels: Elsevier, 1957.

Adorno, Theodor W. "Maurice Ravel." In *Anbruch: Monatsschrift für Moderne Musik*, vol. 12, pp. 151 ff. 1930. Reprinted in Adorno, *Moments Musicaux: Neue Gedruckte Aufsätze 1928–1962*. Frankfurt am Main: Suhrkamp Verlag, 1964.

Alajounine, Théophile. "Aphasia and Artistic Realization." *Brain* (September 1948), 229ff.

Albaret, Céleste. *Monsieur Proust, souvenirs recueillis par Georges Belmont*. Paris: Robert Laffont, 1973.

Alvar-Harding, Charles. "Maurice Ravel Away from his Music." *Musical Courrier* (May 20, 1933).

Aprahamian, Felix. "'L'Heure Espagnole' and 'L'Enfant et les Sortilèges.'" In *Opera on Record 3*, edited by Alan Blyth. Dover, New Hampshire: Longwood Press, 1984.

Aubin, Tony et al. *Maurice Ravel*. Paris: Les Publications Techniques et Artistiques, 1945.

Barbey D'Aurevilly, Jules. *Du Dandysme et de George Brummel.* Edited by Marie-Christine Natta. Malakoff, France: Plein chant, 1989.

Barthes, Roland. *Fragments d'un discours amoureux.* Paris: Seuil, 1973.

Bartley, W. W., III. *Wittgenstein.* 2nd ed. La Salle, Illinois: Open Court Paperbacks, 1985.

Bauer, Harold. *His Book.* New York: Norton, 1948.

Benedictus, Louis. *Les Musiques bizarres à l'Exposition de 1900.* Paris: Olendorff, 1900. (sixth brochure, "Les Chants de Madagascar," transcribed by Benedictus.)

Bennett, Arnold. *The Glimpse.* London: Appleton, 1909.

———. *The Journal of Arnold Bennett.* London: The Literary Guild, 1933.

Bentivoglio, Leonetta. "Danza e futurismo in Italia: 1913–1930." *La Danza Italiana,* 1 (Autumn 1984): 68–69.

Berkeley, Lennox. "Maurice Ravel." *ADAM* 41 (1978): 13ff.

Bertholet, Denis. *Paul Valéry 1871–1945.* Paris: Plon, 1995.

Beucler, André. *Vingt ans avec Léon-Paul Fargue.* Editions du milieu du Monde, Paris 1952. (To be avoided is the abridged English translation by Geoffrey Sainsbury, published as *The Last of the Bohemians* (New York: W. Sloane Associates 1954) most recently reprinted by Greenwood Press, 1970, and anthologized.)

Böhm, Karl. *Ma Vie.* Translated by Elisabeth Bouillon. Paris: Lattès, 1980.

Boivin, Jean. *La Classe de Messiaen.* Paris: Christian Bourgois, 1995.

Boney-Maury, P., and J. de Herdt, *Judo et Jiu-Jitsu.* Paris: Vigot frères, 1949.

Borgeaud, Philippe. *The Cult of Pan in Ancient Greece.* Translated from the French by Kathleen Arthur and James Redfield, University of Chicago Press, 1988.

Brand, Juliane, et al. *The Berg-Schoenberg Correspondence: Selected Letters.* New York: Norton, 1987.

Bruyr, José. *Maurice Ravel.* Paris: Plon, 1950.

Buckle, Richard. *Nijinsky.* New York: Avon Books, 1971.

Cahiers Maurice Ravel, volumes 1–5, 1985–1992. Paris: Fondation Maurice Ravel.

Calvocoressi, Michel. *Musicians Gallery: Music and Ballet in Paris and London.* London: Faber & Faber, 1933

———. "Ravel's Letters to Calvocoressi." *Musical Quarterly* 27 (January 1941), 1ff.

Calza, Renato. *Maurice Ravel nella storia della critica: poetiche Decadenti Ravelliane e interpretazioni novecentesche in Francia, Italia, Inghilterra, e Stati Uniti.* Milano: Ed. G. Zanibon, 1980.

———. *I prestigi della notte: Gaspard de la Nuit tra Aloysius Bertrand e Maurice Ravel,* Treviso, Ass. Musicale "Ensemble 1900," c. 1994.

Carley, Lionel. *Delius: A Life in Letters I, 1862–1908.* Cambridge, Massachusetts: Harvard University Press, 1983.

Casadesus, Robert. "Memories of Ravel." *Musical America* (February 10, 1941), 221ff.

Chalupt, René, and Marcelle Gerar. *Ravel au miroir de ses lettres.* Paris: Robert Laffont, 1956.

Clerget, M., et al. *Les Merveilles de l'Exposition de 1889.* 2 vols. Paris: La Librairie Illustrée. 1889.

Cocteau, Jean. *Past Tense.* vol. 2: *Diaries.* Edited by Pierre Chanel and translated from the French by Richard Howard. New York: Harcourt Brace, 1988.

———. *Lettres à André Gide.* Paris: La Table Ronde, 1970.

Cocteau, Jean, and Jacques-Emile Blanche. *Correspondance.* Paris: La Table Ronde, 1993.

Colette. *Au Concert.* Edited by Alain Galliari. Paris: Le Castor Astral, 1992.

———. *La jumelle noire.* Paris: Fayard, 1991.

Copland, Aaron. *The New Music 1900–1960.* New York: Norton, 1968.

Copley, Anthony. *Sexual Moralities in France, 1780–1980: New Ideas on the Family, Divorce, and Homosexuality—An essay on moral change.* London and New York: Routledge, 1989.

Coppola, Piero. *Dix-Sept Ans de musique à Paris.* Lausanne: F. Rouge, 1944.

Cortambert, Louise. *Le Langage des Fleurs.* Paris: Garnier Frères, 1819.

Cuénod, Hugues. Unpublished correspondence with the author, January 9, 1997.

DeGraff, Amy Vanderlyn. *The Tower and the Well: A Psychological Interpretation of the Fairy Tales of Madame d'Aulnoy.* Birmingham, Alabama: Summa, 1984.

Del Mar, Norman. *A Companion to the Orchestra.* London: Faber, 1987.

Delteil, Joseph. *Jeanne d'Arc.* Paris: Grasset, 1925. (There is an English translation by Malcolm Cowley. New York: Minton, Balch, & Co., 1926.)

Demuth, Norman. *Ravel.* London: J. M. Dent, 1947.

Diamond, David. Interview with author at Juilliard School of Music, New York City, 1997.

Dickinson, Peter. *The Music of Lennox Berkeley.* London: Thames Publishing, 1988.

Diehl, Gaston, et al. *Henri Manguin 1874–1949.* Paris: Musée Marmottan, 1988.

Dotoli, Giovanni. *Lo Scrittore Totale: Saggi su Ricciotto Canudo.* Fasano: Schena, 1986.

Du Bos, Charles. *Journal IX, avril 1934–février 1939.* Paris: La Colombe, 1961.

Dumesnil, Maurice. "Maurice Ravel." *The Etude* (September 1934).

Dunfee, Norman V. "Maurice Ravel in America 1928." Ph.D. diss., University of Missouri, Kansas City, 1980.

Durand, Jacques. *Quelques souvenirs d'un éditeur de musique.* Paris: Durand & Co, 1924.

L'Exposition 1889 chez soi. Paris: L. Boulanger, 1889.

Falla, Manuel de. *Escritos sobre musica y musicos.* Madrid: Espasa-Calpe, 1988. (There is a French translation by Jean-Dominique Krynen. Arles, France: Actes Sud, 1992.

Fargue, Léon-Paul. *Maurice Ravel.* Paris: Domat, 1949.

———. *Refuges.* Paris: Emile-Paul frères, 1942.

Faucigny-Lucinge, Jean-Louis de. *Un Gentilhomme cosmopolite.* Paris: Perrin, 1990.

Février, Jacques. "Les Exigences de Ravel." *Revue Internationale de Musique* (April 1939), 893ff.

Flanner, Janet. *Paris Was Yesterday.* Edited by Irving Drutman. New York: Viking Press, 1972.

Fokine, Michel. *Memoirs of a Ballet Master.* Boston: Little Brown, 1961.

Garafola, Lynn. *Diaghilev's Ballets Russes.* Oxford University Press, 1989.

Gassier, Pierre. *Manguin parmi les Fauves.* Martigny, Switzerland: Fondation Pierre Gianadda, 1983.

Gauthier, Eva. "Reminiscences of Maurice Ravel." *New York Times,* January 16, 1938.

Gavazzeni, Gianandrea. "L'Opera che Ravel non Scrissi." *La Scala* (May 1951), 29ff. (The title refers to the project *Le Grand Meaulnes.*)

Giroire, Henri. *Clovis Vincent (1879–1947): Pionnier de la Neurochirugie Française.* Paris: Olivier Perrin, 1971.

Goss, Madeleine. *Bolero: The Life of Maurice Ravel.* New York: Henry Holt, 1940.

Greilsammer, Ilan. *Blum.* Paris: Flammarion, 1996.

Gubisch, Nina. "Le Journal inédit de Ricardo Viñes." *Revue internationale de musique française* (June 1980): 154ff.

———. "Ricardo Viñes à travers son journal et sa correspondance." Ph.D. diss., Université de Paris IV—La Sorbonne, 1977. (The thousand-page "Journal of Ricardo Viñes," most of which is still unpublished, remains in the private collection of his heirs.)

Guilleminault, Gilbert, and André Mahé. *L'Epopée de la révolte: le roman vrai d'un siècle d'anarchie (1862–1962).* Paris: Denoël 1963.

Guitard, Louis. "Sur trois lettres de Paul Morand." In *Paul Morand Ecrivain,* ed. Michel Colomb. Montpellier: Université Paul-Valéry, 1993.

Guitard-Auviste, Ginette. *Paul Morand (1888–1976): Légendes et vérités*. Paris: Balland, 1994.

Gury, Christian. *L'Extravagant Maurice Rostand: un ami de Proust et de Cocteau*. Paris: Kimé, 1994.

Hearne, Betsy. *Beauty and the Beast: Visions and Revisions of an Old Tale*. Chicago: University of Chicago Press, 1989.

Hepburn, James G. *The Art of Arnold Bennett*. Bloomington: Indiana University Press, 1964.

Hepburn, James, G., ed. *Letters of Arnold Bennett, vol. 2, 1889–1915*. Oxford University Press, 1968.

Herresthal, Harald, and Ladislav Reznicek. *Rhapsodie norvégienne: Les musiciens norvégiens en France au temps de Grieg*, trans. Chantal de Batz. Caen: Presses Universitaires de Caen, 1994.

Hirsbrunner, Theo. *Maurice Ravel, sein Leben, sein Werk*. Laaber: Laaber-Verlag, 1989.

Hofmannsthal, Christiane von. *Tagebücher 1918–1923*. Edited by Maya Rauch and Gerhard Schuster. Frankfurt am Main: S. Fischer Verlag, 1991.

Hofmannsthal, Hugo von. "Gesammelte Werke in Zwölf Einzelausgaben. Vol. 3, prosa IV. Frankfurt am Main: S. Fischer Verlag, 1955.

Hofmannsthal, Hugo von, and Harry Graf Kessler. *Briefwechsel 1898–1929*. Edited by Hilde Burge. Frankfurt am Main: Insel Verlag, 1968.

Hogg, James. *James Elroy Flecker's "Hassan": A Near-Masterpiece*. Salzburg: Institut Für Englische Sprache, 1975.

Honegger-Moyse, Blanche. Unpublished correspondence with author, 23 February 1997.

Houssaye, Henry. *Histoire d'Alcibiade et de la république athéni-enne.* Paris: Didier et cie., 1874.

Huas, Jeanine. *L'Homosexualité au temps de Proust.* Dinard: Danclau, 1992.

Irwin, Robert. *The Arabian Nights: A Companion.* New York: Penguin, 1994.

Jacques-Chaquin, Nicole. *Tableau de l'inconstance des mauvais anges et démons.* Edited by Pierre de Lancre. 1612. Reprint. Paris: Aubier, 1982.

Jankélévitch, Vladimir. *Ravel.* Paris: Seuil, 1996.

Jean-Aubry, Georges. *La Musique française d'aujourd'hui.* Paris: Perrin & Co., 1916.

———. "Profils perdus—Maurice Ravel. *Le Censeur Politique et Littéraire* (July 20, 1907).

———. "Maurice Ravel," *Chesterian* 19 (1938) 65ff.

Jourdan-Morhange, Hélène. *Ravel et nous.* Paris: Editions du milieu du monde, 1945.

Kessler, Harry. *The Diaries of a Cosmopolitan: Count Harry Kessler 1918–1937.* Translated and edited by Charles Kessler. London: Weidenfeld, 1971.

Klingsor, Tristan. "Les Musiciens et les poètes contemporains." *Mercure de France* (November 1900) 430ff.

Lacretelle, Jacques de. *Journal de Bord.* Paris: Grasset, 1974.

Lemaire, Michel. *Le Dandysme de Baudelaire à Mallarmé.* Montreal: Les Presses de l'Université de Montréal, 1978.

Léon, Georges. *Maurice Ravel.* Paris: Seghers, 1964.

Lesure, François. *Maurice Ravel.* Paris: Bibliothèque Nationale, 1975.

————. *Claude Debussy: Biographie critique*. Paris: Klincksieck, 1994.

Lévi-Strauss, Claude. *Regarder Ecouter Lire*. Paris: Plon, 1993.

Lévy, Mischa. "Ravel as the Molière of Music." *Musical America* (February 28, 1920). The article is an interview with the composer, conducted in 1919.)

Levy, Suzy. *Journal inédit de Ricardo Viñes: Odilon Redon et le milieu occultiste (1897–1915)*. Paris: Aux Amateurs des Livres, 1987.

Levy, Suzy, ed. *Lettres inédites d'Odilon Redon à Bonger, Jourdain, Viñes*. Paris: José Corti, 1987.

Lewis, Laurence. *Guido Cantelli: Portrait of a Maestro*. San Diego: A. S. Barnes & Co., 1981.

Long, Marguérite. *Au piano avec Maurice Ravel*. Paris: Julliard, 1971.

McGuinness, Brian. *Wittgenstein: A Life, Young Ludwig 1889–1921*. London: G. Duckworth, 1988.

MacLeod, Joseph. *The Sisters d'Aranyi*. London: Allen & Unwin, 1969.

Mahler-Werfel, Alma. *Mein Leben*. Frankfurt am Main: S. Fischer Verlag, 1960. (This German edition makes important additions to Alma's English-language memoir, *And the Bridge is Love*, written in collaboration with E. B. Ashton and published by Harcourt Brace in New York: 1958.)

Marcel, Gabriel. *L'Esthetique musicale de Gabriel Marcel*. Paris: Aubier, Association Présence de Gabriel Marcel, 1980.

Marnat, Marcel. *Maurice Ravel*. Paris: Fayard, 1986.

Marnat, Marcel, ed. *Ravel: Souvenirs de Maurice Rosenthal*. Paris: Hazan, 1995.

Martin, Frank. "Maurice Ravel ou le paradoxe du compositeur." *Revue Musicale Suisse* (18 March 1938). Reprinted in Frank Martin, *Un compositeur médite sur son art.* Neuchâtel: Editions de la Baconnière, 1977.

Maurer, Warren. *Understanding Gerhart Hauptmann.* Columbia, S.C.: University of South Carolina Press, 1992.

Migliore, Sandra. *Tra Hermes e Promoteo: Il Mito di Leonardo nel Decadentismo Europeo.* Firenze: Leo S. Olschki, 1994.

Milhaud, Darius. *Notes sans musique.* Paris: Julliard, 1949.

Milstein, Nathan, and Solomon Volkov. *From Russia to the West: The Musical Memoirs and Reminiscences of Nathan Milstein.* Translated by Antonina Bovis. New York: Henry Holt, 1990.

Moldenhauer, Hans, and Rosaleen Moldenhauer. *Anton von Webern: A Chronicle of his Life and Work.* New York: Alfred A. Knopf, 1979.

Monk, Ray. *Ludwig Wittgenstein, The Duty of Genius.* London: Jonathan Cape, 1990.

Monteux, Doris. *Everyone is Someone: the Memoirs of Fifi Monteux.* New York: Farrar Straus & Cudahy, 1962.

———. *It's All in the Music: The Life and Work of Pierre Monteux.* New York: Farrar Straus & Giroux, 1965.

Morelli, Giovanni. *Alfredo Casella negli Anni di Apprendistato a Parigi.* Firenze: Leo S. Olschki, 1994.

Munro, John M. *James Elroy Flecker.* Boston: Twayne Publishers, 1976.

Myers, Rollo. *Ravel.* London: G. Duckworth, 1960.

Narbaitz, Pierre. *Maurice Ravel: un orfèvre basque.* (s.l.) Côte Basque, 1975.

Nichols, Roger. *Ravel*. London: J. M. Dent, 1977.

———. *Ravel Remembered*. London: Faber & Faber 1987.

Orenstein, Arbie. *Maurice Ravel: Lettres, Ecrits, Entretiens*. Paris: Flammarion, 1989.

———. *A Ravel Reader*. New York: Columbia University Press, 1990.

———. *Ravel: Man and Musician*. New York: Dover, 1991.

Painter, George. *Marcel Proust*. London: Chatto & Windus, 1965.

Pannain, Guido. *Musicisti dei Tempi Nuovi*. Torino: G. B. Paravia, 1932. (Translated with a note by Michael R. Bonavia, as Modern Composers. London: J. M. Dent, 1932.)

Perlemuter, Vlado, and Hélène Jourdan-Morhange. *Ravel d'après Ravel*. Lausanne: Editions du Cervin, 1970.

Piatigorsky, Gregor. *Cellist*. Garden City, New York: Doubleday, 1965.

Pirlot, Gérard, et al. *Les Mille et une Nuits: contes sans frontières*. Toulouse: AMAM, 1994.

Piston, Danièle, ed. *Maurice Ravel au XXième siècle, Table Ronde Internationale organisée à l'occasion du centenaire de sa naissance*. Paris: CNCM, 1976.

Pizzetti, Ildebrando. *Musicisti Contemporanei*. Milano: Fratelli Treves, 1914.

Poe, Edgar Allan. *Poems and Essays on Poetry*. Edited by C. H. Sisson. London: Fyfield Books, Carcanet, 1995.

Porel, Jacques. *Fils de Réjane: Souvenirs vol. 1 (1895–1920), vol. 2 (1920–1950)*. Paris: Plon, 1951.

Poulenc, Francis. *Moi et mes amis*. Paris: La Palatine, 1963.

————. *Correspondance.* Edited by Myriam Chimènes. Paris: Fayard, 1994.

Proust, Marcel. *Correspondance.* vol. 9, 14, 17. Paris: Plon, 1982.

Ravel, Maurice. "Letters to Lucien Garban and others." In a catalogue (prepared by Laurin-Guilloux, Buffetard, and Tailleur) for an auction of letters and musical manuscripts, held at the Salle Drouot in Paris on April 8, 1992.

Renard, Jules. *Journal 1887–1910.* Edited by Léon Guichard. Paris: Gallimard, 1960.

Restout, Denise, ed. *Landowska on Music.* New York: Stein & Day, 1964.

Robinson, Harlow. *Sergey Prokofiev.* New York: Viking, 1987.

Roland-Manuel. *Maurice Ravel et son oeuvre.* Paris: Durand & Co., 1914.

————. *Maurice Ravel et son oeuvre dramatique.* Paris: Les Editions Musicales de la Librarie de France, 1928.

————. *À la gloire de Ravel.* Paris: Editions de la Nouvelle Revue Critique, 1938.

————. *Ravel.* Paris: Gallimard, 1948.

Rorem, Ned. "Historic Houses: Maurice Ravel at Le Belvédère." *Architectural Digest* (September 1986), 182ff.

Rosen, Carole. *The Goossens: A Musical Century.* London: André Deutsch, 1993.

Rosen, Charles. "Where Ravel Ends and Debussy Begins." *Cahiers Debussy* 3 (1979): 34.

Roy, Jean, ed. *Maurice Ravel: Lettres à Roland-Manuel et à sa famille.* Paris: Caligrammes, 1986.

Rubinstein, Arthur. *My Young Years.* New York: Alfred A. Knopf, 1973.

———. *My Many Years.* New York: Alfred A. Knopf, 1980.

Sachs, Harvey. *Rubinstein: A Life.* New York: Grove Press, 1995.

Salazar, Adolfo. *"Musica y Musicos de Hoy: ensayos sobre la musica Actual.* Madrid: Editorial Mundo Latino, 1928.

Sams, Jeremy. "Ravel." In *Songs on Record 2,* ed. Alan Blyth. Cambridge University Press, 1988.

Santomauro, Maria. *El Gracioso en el Teatro de Tirso de Molina.* Madrid: edita Revista 'Estudios,' Madrid, 1984 (published version of author's Ph.D. diss., the City University of New York).

Seaton, Beverly. *The Language of Flowers: A History.* Charlottesville: University Press of Virginia, 1995.

Seibert, Kurt, et al. *Hommage à Ravel 1987.* Bremen: Hochschule für gestaltende Kunst und Musik, 1987.

Serge, Victor. *Mémoires d'un révolutionnaire.* Paris: Seuil, 1951.

Seroff, Victor. *Maurice Ravel.* New York: Henry Holt, 1953.

Sert, Misia. *Misia.* Paris: Gallimard, 1952.

Sherwood, John. *No Golden Journey: A Biography of James Elroy Flecker.* London: Heinemann 1973.

Slonimsky, Nicolas. *Perfect Pitch: A Life Story.* London and New York: Oxford University Press, 1988.

Stravinsky, Igor. *Selected Correspondence.* vol. 3, ed. Robert Craft. New York: Alfred A. Knopf, 1985.

Stravinsky, Vera, and Robert Craft. *Stravinsky in Pictures and Documents.* New York: Simon & Schuster, 1978.

Stuckenschmidt, H. H. *Maurice Ravel: Variations on his Life and Work.* Translated by Samuel Rosenbaum. Philadelphia: Chilton Books, 1968.

Szigeti, Joseph. *With Strings Attached: Reminiscences and Reflections.* New York: Alfred A. Knopf, 1967.

Tawaststjerna, Erik. *Sibelius.* vol 2: 1904–1914. Translated by Robert Layton. Berkeley: University of California Press, 1986.

Tertis, Lionel. *My Viola and I: A Complete Autobiography.* London: Paul Elek, 1974.

Thibault, Claude. *Un Million de Judokas: Histoire de Judo Français.* Paris: Albin Michel, 1966.

Thomson, Virgil. *Music Reviewed 1940–1954.* New York: Vintage, 1966.

Valéry, Paul. *Cahiers.* 2 vols. Edited by Judith Robinson-Valéry. Paris: Gallimard, 1974.

Williams, Ursula Vaughan. *RVW: A Biography of Ralph Vaughan Williams.* New York: Oxford University Press, 1964.

Villeneuve, Roland. *Le Fléau des sorciers: la diablerie basque au XVIIe siècle.* Paris: Flammarion, 1983.

Vuillermoz, Emile, et al. *Maurice Ravel par quelques-uns de ses familiers.* Paris: Editions du Tambourinaire, 1939.

Zaccono, Pierre. *Nouveau langage des fleurs.* Paris: Hachette, 1858.

Index

About the Author

Benjamin Ivry is a poet, translator, and author who has written critically acclaimed biographies of Arthur Rimbaud (Absolute Press/Stewart, Tabori & Chang) and Francis Poulenc (Phaidon). His poetry collection, *Paradise for the Portugese Queen,* was published by Orchises Press, and his translation, in collaboration with Renata Gorczynski, of a book of poems by Adam Zagajewski, *Canvas,* appeared from Farrar Straus & Giroux/Faber & Faber. He has also translated and abridged Olivier Todd's life of Albert Camus for Alfred A. Knopf/ Jonathan Cape publishers. Mr. Ivry, who is based in Manhattan, writes, lectures, and broadcasts widely on the arts.